Proofreading & Editing

Grade 5

Published by Instructional Fair
an imprint of

 **Children's Publishing**

Author: Kelly Hatfield and Rob Hatfield
Project Director/Editor: Kathryn Wheeler
Editor: Diana Wallis

Children's Publishing

Published by Instructional Fair
An imprint of McGraw-Hill Children's Publishing
Copyright © 2004 McGraw-Hill Children's Publishing

Send all inquiries to:
McGraw-Hill Children's Publishing
3195 Wilson Drive NW
Grand Rapids, Michigan 49544

Proofreading & Editing—grade 5
ISBN: 0-7424-2755-2

1 2 3 4 5 6 7 8 9 MAL 09 08 07 06 05 04

Table of Contents

Name _____   Date _____

Mark It, Change It

Authors and editors use special marks to proofread and edit. These are called **proofreading marks**. These marks show how to fix mistakes. When you edit and proofread, you can use these marks, too. They are fast and easy to use.

1. Here is the mark to make a capital letter: <u>a</u>.

   example: I live in <u>columbus</u>, Ohio.

   Mark this sentence to fix the letters that should be capitals

   when I was six, my family drove to san francisco.

2. Here is the mark to change a capital letter into a lowercase letter: ‎G̸ .

   example: We are G̸oing to California again.

   Mark this sentence to fix the letters that should be lowercase.

   This time, I want to go across The Golden Gate Bridge.

3. Here is the mark to delete, or take out, a word: ℓ .

   example: We are going to stay with Aunt Maria and and Uncle Miguel.

   Mark this sentence to take out the extra word.

   After we see San Francisco, we are will going to Los Angeles.

4. To fix letters that are in the wrong order, use this mark: ∩ .

   example: We are going to stay with Aunt Maria and Ucnle Miguel.

   Mark this sentence to fix the misspelled word.

   Mom says that travle helps people learn.

4   0-7424-2755-2 *Proofreading & Editing*

Mark It, Change It (cont.)

5.   Here is the mark to put something into a sentence: ︿

When you add a comma, put it inside the mark: ︿

    example: My dad also wants to go to Laguna Beach︿Monterey Bay, and
                            San Diego on this trip.

When you add a word, a period, a question mark, a quotation mark, or an exclamation mark,
use the mark to show the place. Then write the word or punctuation mark above it.

    example: My dad also wants to go to ︿ on this trip.
                                 San Diego

Put the missing punctuation and words into this sentence.

     Los Angeles is huge bright busy

6.   Here is the mark to show the start of a new paragraph: ¶

    example: ¶ Today, we start driving home.

Use the paragraph mark to show where the new paragraph starts.

     Last year, my summer vacation was boring. We stayed at home and went on a few short

trips. Time really dragged. This summer, my family and I are driving to San Francisco! Then

we will drive down the state to Los Angeles. We will go to Disneyland and see the studios

in Hollywood.

Now use the proofreading marks you have learned to edit these sentences.

7.   Aunt maria will cook Seafood for us

8.   I want buy my mom a Map of California, so we can plan our trip?

                  0-7424-2755-2 *Proofreading & Editing*

Endings in Space

When you are editing punctuation, remember:

A **statement** ends with a **period** (.).

Kathy and Leopold work on the space station *Deep Alpha*.

A **question** ends with a **question mark** (?).

Do you know about it**?**

An **exclamation** ends with an **exclamation point** (!).

The life-support system went out**!**

A **command** can end with a **period** or an **exclamation point**.

Call for help**!**

Find the reboot button**.**

This is the mark to add punctuation: .

Mark the sentences to add the missing punctuation.

1. Kathy and Leopold entered the capsule

2. What is their mission

3. Look out   It's an asteroid

4. Kathy calls back to the ship

5. They are on their way into deep space

Becky wrote a story about Kathy and Leopold in space. Proofread her story opening and put in the missing punctuation. Use this mark γ to take out punctuation that is wrong.

6.   Leopold knew? that the first stay in the capsule was hard on new people He double-

checked the life-support system, placed the glass-domed helmet on his head, and locked

it into place. As he nodded and moved through the airlock, Kathy closed the inner door

behind him "I guess there's no going back now, right" she asked Leopold just shrugged

6   0-7424-2755-2 *Proofreading & Editing*

Name _____   Date _____

Mission Punctuation

Editors must check the punctuation inside sentences.
Here are some ways that **commas** are used:

in **dates**:	November 4, 2025
in **addresses**:	Cape Canaveral, Florida
in a **series**:	helmets, gloves, and space boots

in **prepositional phrases**: Before the launch, they checked their seat belts.

in **compound sentences** before the conjunction:

Leopold tapped his fingers, and Kathy looked out the porthole.

Use this mark to add a comma:

Use this mark to take out a comma:

Quotation marks show the speaker's exact words.

Put quotations marks outside of the punctuation that is included in the quote.

Capitalize the first word of the quote, unless the quote is the second part of a sentence.

Separate a quote from the rest of the sentence with a comma, a question mark, or an exclamation point.

"**H**ow long will it take us to get to the outer moon?" asked Kathy.

"**A**bout two days," Leopold replied. "**I**t's an easy trip!"

Place commas in these sentences.

1. Kathy ducked to enter the capsule and Leopold followed her.

2. After a few minutes Leopold entered the control room.

3. Kathy made sure the door was shut locked and secure.

4. Leopold opened a metal box took out a connector and plugged it in.

Punctuate these sentences correctly including quotation marks.

5. I feel as though I'm going into a giant tin can " complained Kathy.

6. "You'll get used to it said Leopold "after you've been on a few trips.

The Explorers

Use this mark to add punctuation: ⌃"Watch out!"⌃
Use this mark to take out incorrect punctuation.
Lewis started his hike up the hill?

1. Use proofreading marks to correct the punctuation in this story.

Meriwether Lewis waded through piles of dead leaves that were sometimes as deep as his knees He had been high above the river for the last two hours and he was now able to see a long way. There they are he said to himself as he watched the others in their small boat below him Lewis checked his bearings. The river seems to be flowing due west he said I must add that to my sketch He also added a line of mountains far to the north another river flowing in from the south and the red-rock cliffs

Far to the west a heavy bank of clouds loomed on the horizon Lewis had been watching them for days That main cloud bank never moves he said to himself. He was sure there was a great ocean just beyond the clouds There has to be he told himself.

He started his hike back down to the river The cold winds were starting to pick up and he wanted to be close to camp by dusk Clark would have camp set up. Their guide would be cooking the evening meal

2. Write three more sentences about Lewis and Clark or another explorer. Be sure to use correct punctuation.

_____

_____

_____

_____

The Iroquois

Names are always capitalized.

    Canassatego went to Philadelphia.

Titles are capitalized if they are used in front of a name.

    Chief Canassatego was an important person.

If the title follows the name, it is not capitalized.

    Canassatego was a **c**hief in 1744.

Names of places are capitalized.

    The state of **N**ew **Y**ork was the center of the Iroquois nation.

The names of **days** and **months** are always capitalized.

    Monday   June 12

This is the mark to capitalize a letter: <u>a</u>lgonquin

This is the mark to turn a capital letter into a lowercase letter: T̸reaty

Circle the choice that shows correct capitalization.

1.   a. chen read about

     b. the Culture

     c. of the Iroquois.

2.   a. The iroquois

     b. were Native Americans who

     c. lived in New York and pennsylvania.

3.   a. the Nation of the iroquois

     b. was very Powerful

     c. in this region.

Mark the sentences to correct the capitalization.

4.   The iroquois, the mahicans, and the Wampanoag all lived in eastern america.

5.   All the chiefs of the iroquois people were at the meeting.

6.   Native americans hunted and harvested Food in the Fall each year.

7.   We will be having a test on friday, February 13.

8.   mr. lehman told us about the Longhouses of the Iroquois.

9.   In lancaster, Pennsylvania, the tribes met in june of 1744.

10. Benjamin franklin read the iroquois Treaty.

Capping It Off

Titles and **subheads** are capitalized. Only the main words in a title are capitalized. Verbs are always capitalized, even if they are short words. The first and last words of a title are always capitalized.

Sarah, Plain and Tall   *The History of the Iroquois Nation*

This is the mark to capitalize a letter: <u>a</u>lgonquin.

This is the mark to turn a capital letter into a lowercase letter : /.

My Vacation A̸t the Beach

Circle the choice that shows the right capitalization.

1. a. *Harry Potter And The Order Of The Phoenix*

   b. *Harry Potter and the Order of the Phoenix*

   c. *Harry Potter and The Order of The Phoenix*

2. a. *My Dog is from Pluto*

   b. *My dog Is from pluto*

   c. *My Dog Is from Pluto*

3. a. *Tuck Everlasting*

   b. *Tuck EverLasting*

   c. *Tuck everlasting*

4. a. *Harriet The Spy*

   b. *Harriet the Spy*

   c. *Harriet The spy*

5. a. *Island of The Blue Dolphins*

   b. *Island Of The Blue Dolphins*

   c. *Island of the Blue Dolphins*

6. a. *The Westing game*

   b. *The Westing Game*

   c. *the Westing Game*

7. Use proofreading marks to correct the capitalization in the paragraph.

Our book reports are due tomorrow. I read *the Boggart* by Susan Cooper. Janna read *the Indian in The Cupboard.* Kristin liked *The Princess bride.* There are so many great books to read! I have trouble picking just one.

                   0-7424-2755-2 Proofreading & Editing

The Students Vote

Editors must make sure that all words are capitalized correctly.

This is the mark to capitalize a letter: Native american.

This is the mark to turn a capital letter into a lowercase letter: /.

A Wrinkle In Time

1. Dylan wrote an article for the class newsletter. Use proofreading marks to fix the capitalization mistakes in his report.

Students vote for Favorite Music

The Students have spoken! Last Winter, the students voted to have Music played in the Cafeteria during lunch on fridays. soon after, the question was asked: "what kind of music do students want?"

Students gave ideas to make a ballot. classical, oldies, Country, and rock were put on the ballot. Principal pecoraro said she would respect the Students' choice. she also said that she had her own likes and dislikes. The students voted to have the teachers and the Principal vote, too.

Voting took place on thursday at lunch. There were 245 students who voted. students from the sixth grade counted the Votes. you can hear the results every friday at lunch!

Circle the choice that shows the right capitalization.

2. a. tuesday, january 22
   b. tuesday, January 22
   c. Tuesday, January 22

3. a. Our teacher is mr. Coviak.
   b. Our Teacher is Mr. Coviak.
   c. Our teacher is Mr. Coviak.

4. a. *The house on the hill*
   b. *The House on the Hill*
   c. *The House On the Hill*

5. a. Police Chief Harry Martinez
   b. Police Chief Harry martinez
   c. Police chief Harry Martinez

Name _____ Date _____

Spelling Counts

Editors must check the spelling in each piece of writing that they proofread. They use a dictionary if they are not sure how a word is spelled.

Circle the choice that shows the right spelling.

1. _____ is wrong here.
   a. Sumthing
   b. Some thing
   c. something
   d. Sum Thing

2. My _____ music is jazz.
   a. favrite
   b. faverite
   c. favarite
   d. favorite

3. We _____ finished the test.
   a. finely
   b. finelly
   c. finally
   d. finaly

4. _____ house is white with a blue roof.
   a. Or
   b. Hour
   c. Oure
   d. Our

Read each phrase. Choose the phrase in which the underlined word is not spelled correctly for the way it is used in the phrase.

5. a. worldwide <u>piece</u>
   b. <u>idle</u> behavior
   c. wounds will <u>heal</u>
   d. light the <u>flare</u>

6. a. $50 <u>fare</u>
   b. <u>lesson</u> learned
   c. <u>fowl</u> ball
   d. apple <u>core</u>

7. a. <u>write</u> a message
   b. <u>herd</u> of buffalo
   c. results will <u>vary</u>
   d. tie a <u>not</u>

Rewrite these words correctly on the lines.

8. evirament_____

9. comunity _____

10. hitstory _____

0-7424-2755-2 Proofreading & Editing

Invisible Ink

When you proofread, it is important to look for spelling mistakes. You can use proofreading marks to fix them.

If there is just one extra letter, use this mark to take it out: frieend .

If the word is spelled wrong, use the same mark to take out the whole word. Then write the correct spelling above it.

mineral
minaral

If the letters are in the wrong order, use this mark to fix them: recieve.

1. Proofread the following paragraphs for misspelled words. Use proofreading marks to fix the spelling mistakes.

Have you ever wanted to shair a secret with someone without anyone else knowing? Hears a way you can write secret messages. You can share seecrets with a freind without anyone else noing what you've written! It's easy and fun too do.

First, you will need a fresh lemon, a toothpick, and some white paper. Your freind will need an oven to read your message.

Start bye squeezing the jooce from the lemon into a small bole. Next, use the toothpick two write your secret message. Use the lemon juice as ink. When the "ink" is drie, the mesage will be almost invisible!

Here is how your freind can reed the message. This step requires heet. Have your friend ask an adult too put the paper in the oven. The oven shud be heated to 350 degrees for ate to ten minutes. The heat will react with the lemon juice. This will make your mesage appear!

Rewrite these words correctly on the lines.

2. squeaze _____

3. mesege _____

4. thru _____

5. thay _____

6. leter _____

7. acktual _____

Changing Words

Sometimes editors must change one word to another. Sometimes an editor will do this to make a sentence simpler or easier to read or to make the sentence sound better. Editors must choose **synonyms**, words that mean about the same thing.

Read each phrase. Choose the word that means the same or about the same as the underlined word.

1. successful <u>corporation</u>
    a. business
    b. team
    c. person
    d. country

2. skilled <u>laborer</u>
    a. musician
    b. professor
    c. worker
    d. relative

3. tiny <u>particle</u>
    a. animal
    b. package
    c. piece
    d. gift

4. a desert <u>region</u>
    a. area
    b. culture
    c. religion
    d. plant

5. An <u>imaginary</u> story
    a. biographical
    b. fictional
    c. actual
    d. humorous

Replace the underlined word in the sentence with another word that means about the same. Write your word choice on the line.

6. Buster is an <u>affectionate</u> dog. _____

7. I <u>admire</u> Mrs. Sayer. _____

8. I want to finish my <u>assignment</u>. _____

Being Possessive

Editors must look at lots of things when they look at a piece of writing. One thing they check is that **possessives** are used in the right way.

That book is Michael**'s**. (singular)

We went to our friend**s'** house. (plural)

Some words are plural, but do not end with –s or –es. You make the possessive form of these words with an apostrophe and an –s, as if they were singular.

women**'s** department   children**'s** books

Circle the best phrase to replace the underlined phrase. If the phrase is correct as it is, circle c.

1. Everybody knows that is <u>Ricks' book</u>.
   a. Ricks book
   b. Rick's book
   c. correct as is

2. My dad bought his coat in a <u>mens' store</u>.
   a. men's store
   b. mens store
   c. correct as is

3. This is the <u>twins' birthday party</u>.
   a. twins birthday party
   b. twin's birthday party
   c. correct as is

4. I went to the <u>childrens museum</u>.
   a. childrens' museum
   b. children's museum
   c. correct as is

5. Did you remember your <u>father's birthday</u>?
   a. fathers' birthday
   b. fathers birthday
   c. correct as is

Use proofreading marks to fix the possessives in these sentences.

6. Did you want to go to Marisas house?

7. How was your familys' picnic?

8. I didn't know that she was Mr. Richardsons' daughter!

John Muir, American Hero

When editors proofread, they make sure that each sentence is grammatically correct. If the sentence is not complete, an editor must rewrite it. If the sentence has words in the wrong order, the editor must unscramble them. Each sentence must be clear and easy to read.

Choose the sentence in each group that is grammatically correct.

1.
  a. John Muir was born Scotland in, but grew up in Michigan.

  b. John Muir was born in Scotland but grew up in Michigan.

  c. John Muir born in Scotland, grew up in Michigan.

  d. John Muir was born in Scotland but grew Michigan up in.

2.
  a. John, a child, spent a lot of time outdoors.

  b. When John was a child, he spent outdoors a lot of time.

  c. When John was a child, he spent a lot of time outdoors.

  d. John was a child, and when he spent a lot of time outdoors.

3.
  a. John became of the natural world an explorer.

  b. John became explorer natural world.

  c. John became an natural world explorer.

  d. John became an explorer of the natural world.

4.
  a. The Sierra Nevada California

  b. John's favorite place on Earth was the Sierra Nevada Range in California.

  c. John's favorite place was the Sierra Nevada Range in California on Earth.

  d. John's favorite place, the Sierra Nevada, Range in California, was on Earth.

Rewrite these groups of words to make them grammatically correct sentences.

5. Visited dozens of countries, John.

6. Began writing about nature

7. John's writings inspired to set up many national forests and parks President Roosevelt.

8. Today, millions of people visit thanks to John Muir wilderness areas and enjoy.

The Manta Ray

When editors proofread, they must make sure that each sentence is grammatically correct. If the sentence is a fragment, an editor rewrites it. If the sentence has words in the wrong order, the editor unscrambles them. Sometimes a sentence is missing one or two words.

To fix letters or words that are in the wrong order, use this mark: ∩ .

order wrong

To put something into a sentence, use this mark: ^ .
extra

To take something out of a sentence, use this mark: ℓ .
plus

Use proofreading marks to fix the grammatical mistakes in these sentences.

1. a sea creature over twenty feet wide with horns near its head

2. This "monster" now known is as the gentle and graceful manta ray.

3. The manta ray one member of a large family of fish.

4. The horn shapes near the head of the manta ray guide food into mouth.

5. The manta ray is a giant, it eats only *plankton*, tiny sea plants and animals.

6. Some people call the manta ray "the sea bat," others call it the "devil ray."

7. manta ray long fins that look like wings

8. Its tail moves like a rudder steer to the huge fish through the water.

9. Long ago, sailors thought that the ray manta was a sea monster.

10. spotted the manta ray as it looked for food.

11. As the swam ray through shallow water, the sailors could it see.

12. would like to see a manta ray

The Revolution Is Now!

Editors make sure that verbs in sentences agree with the subjects in number. When verbs are regular, present-tense verbs, you can check them like this:

If the subject is one noun or pronoun (he, she, it), add an **s** to the verb.

George Washington lead**s** the army.

If the subject is **I**, **you**, or **more than one** person, place, or thing, do not add an *s*.

I **see** a redcoat!   The British **shoot** at the colonists.

For the verb **to be**, use **is** for **one** noun or pronoun. Use **are** for **more than one** subject. Use **am** for **I**.

She is an American.   **We are** Americans.   **I am** an American.

Read each sentence aloud. Circle the form of the verb that matches the subject.

1. Boston (is, are) the busiest port in the colonies.

2. The British (march, marches) on Lexington.

3. Paul Revere (warn, warns) that the British are coming.

4. Bunker Hill (is, are) an important battle.

5. In Philadelphia, the Declaration of Independence (is, are) written.

6. John Adams (is, are) one of the authors.

7. So (is, are) Thomas Jefferson.

Use proofreading marks to fix the mistakes in these sentences.

8. My brother join the fighting at Concord.

9. We worries about him as he fights for freedom.

10. Colonists helps each other with food and information.

The Revolution Is Now! (cont.)

When editors look at something in past tense, the subject and verb still have to agree. Most past-tense verbs have **–ed** on the end of the verb. But some verbs are irregular and do not follow the **–ed** rule.

The verb **to be** is one irregular verb. Other examples are **to come, to make, to give,** and **to say**.

Read each sentence aloud. Choose the one in each group in which the subject and verb agree.

11.   a.   Yesterday, Ms. Marlette told us about the Boston Tea Party.

      b.   It was one of the first major rebellions of the war.

      c.   Thousands of pounds of tea was ruined.

12.   a.   Nikita writed a report about the battle of Trenton.

      b.   It took place on Christmas Eve.

      c.   It were a great victory for General Washington.

13.   a.   Benedict Arnold betrayed his country.

      b.   He gived secrets to the British.

      c.   Washington never forgived him for his act.

Use proofreading marks to edit the sentences. Use this mark to take out letters or words that don't belong: ℊ   Use this mark to add words or letters: ∧.

14.   John Paul Jones were a great commander.

15.   General Nathanael Green leaded the army in the South.

16.   Lafayette help the troops after he arrived from France.

17.   Yorktown were the last major battle of the war.

18.   Cornwallis surrender on October 19, 1782.

19.   The Treaty of Paris were signed in 1783.

20.   The brave colonists was now Americans.

21.   On a separate piece of paper write another sentence about the Revolutionary War. Be sure to make subjects and verbs agree.

Arachne

Editors must look for mistakes in grammar as they proofread. When you read a story, use proofreading marks to fix the mistakes.

When you edit, use this mark to add a word or phrase: ∧ .

If there is just one extra letter in a misspelled word, use this mark: letteǝr

If a whole word is wrong, use the same mark to take out the whole word. Then write the correct word above it.

inform
~~form~~

Remember to check that words are used correctly in sentences.
Make sure verbs agree with subjects and that verbs are the right tense.

Use proofreading marks to fix the mistakes in these sentences.

1. Long ago in a distant country live a young woman named Arachne.

2. Arachne weaved the most beautiful cloth anyone had ever seen.

3. Everyone in Arachnes village talked about her wonderful cloth, and soon she

   famous became.

4. But as her fame growed, so did her pride.

5. "I are the best weaver in the world," Arachne boasted.

6. She say, "Not even the goddess Minerva make could anything so fine."

7. Minerva cloth for all the gods

8. She were proud of her weaving and thinked that no human could ever match her skills.

9. Soon Arachne's words reach Minerva's ears and the goddess become angry.

10. Minerva called to Arachne and her challenged to a contest.

Arachne (cont.)

Choose the answer that tells the kind of mistake in each sentence.

11. "Let us both destroy a length of cloth. We will see whose cloth is the best."

    a. wrong word

    b. wrong word order

    c. subject-verb agreement problem

12. set up two looms

    a. wrong word

    b. sentence fragment

    c. subject-verb agreement problem

13. All the villagers watch the contest.

    a. wrong verb tense

    b. double negative

    c. subject-verb agreement problem

14. Look for grammar mistakes in the story. Use proofreading marks to fix them.

The goddesses cloth was all the colors of the rainbow. It sparkled in the sun. It floats on the breeze like a butterfly. But Arachne cloth wove that sparkled like gold and jewels. The villagers was dazzled by Arachne's cloth. When Minerva looks at it, she knew Arachne was the best weaver.

Minerva angry. She taked out a jar of magic water and sprinkled it on Arachne. Instantly, poor Arachne began to change. She become smaller and smaller. She grew more arms. She were covered in fine brown hair. Arachne become had a tiny brown spider. Arachnes' boasting was over. But Minerva let her spend the rest of her life weaving beautiful webs.

21   0-7424-2755-2 Proofreading & Editing

Name _____ Date _____

The Pilgrims

When you proofread, you must check **spelling**, **capitalization**, **punctuation**, and **grammar**. Then use proofreading marks to fix mistakes.

Use this mark to add punctuation or a word: ⌃ .

Use this mark to capitalize a letter: mayflower.

Use this mark to make a capital letter into a lowercase letter: Sailed.

If there is just one extra letter in a word, use this mark: Noveember.

If a word is wrong or spelled wrong, use the same mark to take out the whole word. Then write the word with the right spelling above it.

beginning
~~bagining~~

Use proofreading marks to fix these sentences.

1. The Pilgrims sailed frm Plymouth, England on the *Mayflower* on September 6, 1620.

2. There wes 102 pazzengers on bored.

3. the beginning of the voyage were pleaseant.

4. But then the ship runned into storms and high winds.

5. Beams on deck cracking and let water leak into the ship.

6. Two adults died on the vouyage, and one baby was born, he saw named "Oceanus."

7. On Novmber 9, 1620, the *Mayflower* neared land.

8. It was where is now Cape Cod.

9. Two days later, after 66 days at sea, the ship droped it's anchor.

10. Some of the Pilgrims going ashore.

11. Now we remeber there first harvest celebration on Thankgiving Day.

 0-7424-2755-2 *Proofreading & Editing*

Buster

Alexis is sending a letter to his grandparents. He wants to tell them about his new puppy, Buster. He has asked you to look at the letter before he sends it and to mark any mistakes in capitalization, punctuation, spelling, and grammar.

1.   Use proofreading marks to fix the mistakes in Alexis's letter.

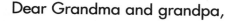

9545 bayview Lane

Dublin, ohio

October 22, 2004

Dear Grandma and grandpa,

I wanted to right to tell you about Buster. Hes my nue puppy! Buster has black fir and big,

pointed ears. He always sniffing arownd. He wants to play all the time and he loves being outside.

dad and I took Buster to the pond. He spend an hour chasing the ducks! Thay where so mad at

him. There was a lot of barking and qacking going on that afternoon

Buster talso go to the ocean last week. he thowt the waves were attacking him. It was sew

funny. He chased the waves back into the see. then he ran back from them when the waves comed

on shore.

Write now, Buster is getting bath. . . in tomatoe joose! Thats' because he surprized a skunk in

our garage Mom says the tomato joose will take out the skunk smell. I shure hope so!

Pleaze write and told me how you are doing. I kin bearly weight for your visit here next month

Buster will be happy to meet you!

your grandson

Alexis

2.   On a separate piece of paper write one more sentence to add to Alexis's letter. Be sure to use correct grammar and spelling.

23   0-7424-2755-2 *Proofreading & Editing*

Poets

A sentence is a group of words with a subject and a predicate and it tells a complete thought. A fragment is not a complete sentence. Editors fix fragments and make them into sentences.

sentences: Shakespeare was a great poet.

                    Robert Frost wrote "The Oven Bird."

                    My favorite poet is Edward Lear.

fragments: Lewis Carroll's monster the Jabberwocky

                    in the poem "The Three Badgers"

                    Because Rudyard Kipling was British

Write **S** on the line before each **sentence**. Write **F** on the line before each **fragment**.

1. _____ "Crows" is a poem by David McCord.

2. _____ Emily Dickinson wrote a poem titled "The Spider."

3. _____ Rhyming words at the end of the line.

4. _____ Because I like to write poetry.

5. _____ T. S. Eliot says that every cat has a secret name.

6. _____ The funny poem "Sir Smasham Uppe."

Read the paragraph. Underline the fragments. Then, rewrite the fragments to make complete sentences. (Hint: Sometimes you can fix a fragment by making it part of another sentence.)

    I love poetry! My favorite author has always been Edward Lear. His poems silly and fun. I have a picture of his owl and pussycat in my room. Now that I'm older, I like to read poems by Robert Frost. Poems set in New England. I like his poem "Mending Wall." I wrote a report about him last week.

7. _____

8. _____

    24   0-7424-2755-2 *Proofreading & Editing*

Animals in the City

Editors sometimes must fix run-on sentences. A **run-on sentence** is two or more sentences that run together without correct punctuation or conjunctions.

    run-on: The squirrel ran it jumped on the bench.

    run-on: The squirrel ran, it jumped on the bench.

    correct: The squirrel ran and jumped on the bench.

               The squirrel ran. It jumped on the bench.

Fix these run-on sentences by writing shorter sentences.

1. Everyone knows that animals and birds live in the forest they also live in cities.

    _____

    _____

2. Squirrels live in trees on city streets, rabbits and oppossums make their homes in the wide-open spaces of city parks.

    _____

    _____

3. Everyone has seen pigeons in the city, they love to flock near fountains and food stands.

    _____

    _____

4. Mice make their nests in apartments, rats find all sorts of hiding places for homes.

    _____

    _____

Fix this run-on sentence by writing a compound sentence. Remember to use both a comma and a conjunction.

5. Raccoons search for food in garbage cans at night, foxes come out at night, too.

    _____

    _____

Paul Revere

Editors make sure that not every sentence is the same. One way they do this is to mix simple, compound, and complex sentences in writing.

A **simple sentence** is **one independent clause**. It has a subject and a predicate and expresses a complete thought.

Paul Revere was a silversmith.

A **compound sentence** has **two independent clauses**.

Revere made silver objects, and he also engraved pictures.

A **complex sentence** has **one independent clause and one or more dependent clauses**. A dependent clause has a subject and predicate, but it is not a complete thought. The dependent clause is underlined in this sentence.

Paul Revere caught his breath <u>as he saw the lanterns in the steeple</u>.

Write an **S** (simple), a **C** (compound), or a **CX** (complex) to show the kind of sentence.

_____ 1. Paul Revere married Sarah Orne, and after her death, he married Rachel Walker.

_____ 2. He was the father of sixteen children.

_____ 3. As Revere worked as a silversmith, he became highly skilled.

_____ 4. Paul Revere was also a patriot.

_____ 5. He knew rebels such as James Otis, and he also was friends with Dr. Joseph Warren.

_____ 6. Because of these ties, Revere helped spread the word about the British treatment of the colonists.

_____ 7. He engraved the famous picture of the Boston Massacre.

_____ 8. Revere made his famous "midnight ride" on April 18, 1775.

_____ 9. He left Boston, and he rode all the way to Lexington.

_____ 10. As Revere watched the battle at Lexington, he was witnessing the start of the Revolutionary War.

The Fourth of July

Editors must make sure that not every sentence is the same. One way they do this is to mix simple, compound, and complex sentences in writing.

A **simple sentence** has one subject and one predicate. It expresses a complete thought. Either the subject or the predicate may be compound.

> I was born on the Fourth of July.   Kim and I lit sparklers.

A **complex sentence** has an independent clause with one subject and one predicate. And it also has a dependent clause that is usually part of the predicate.

> My mom likes the fireworks because they are beautiful.
> Because they are beautiful, my mom likes the fireworks.

A **compound sentence** combines two simple sentences, or independent clauses, with a comma and a conjunction like *or*, *and*, or *but*.

> I like the bands, and my brother likes the decorations.

Circle the subject and underline the predicate in these sentences.

Simple:

1. I like the Fourth of July.

2. The red, white, and blue colors are so bright.

3. My family and I like the parade the best.

Complex:

4. Even though we like the band music, we also like the barbecue after the parade.

5. We always have to wait our turn when we get to the food stand.

6. I like hamburgers the best even though I also like hot dogs.

Compound:

7. The first song is happy, but the second song sounds sad.

8. It reminds Dad of his army friends, and Mom puts her arm around him.

9. It is time for the fireworks, and I can hardly wait!

Pictures in the Mind

Good writing helps the reader see something in his or her mind.
Sometimes editors must replace weak words or phrases with
stronger ones to make that happen.

Jasmine was sad. (weak)

Jasmine's eyes filled with tears. (stronger)

Read each sentence. Look at the underlined word or phrase. Write a stronger word or phrase to replace it on the line below the sentence. Use words that will keep the meaning of the sentence the same.

1. The children <u>said</u>, "We see a ghost."

   _____

2. The worried father <u>walked around</u> the emergency room.

   _____

3. The children <u>walked</u> to school.

   _____

4. The stars <u>were</u> in the sky.

   _____

5. The boy <u>cried</u>.

   _____

6. It is a <u>nice</u> day.

   _____

7. Time <u>moves slowly</u>.

   _____

8. It is a <u>windy</u> day.

   _____

9. Carla <u>put</u> the pan on the stove.

   _____

10. Mr. De Bruyn was <u>tired</u>.

   _____

It's Like This

Sometimes editors must replace weak words or phrases with stronger ones.
An editor can add **similes** to a piece of writing to make it stronger.
Combining two unrelated things creates a vivid picture. When "like"
or "as" is used to make this happen, it is called a *simile*.

She was as frail as an antique clock.

Create stronger sentences by adding a simile to each sentence.

1. I was so tired that I slept like _____.

2. The comet was like a bright _____ shooting through the sky.

3. The lemon drop was as sour as _____.

4. The volcano sat above the town like _____.

5. Priscilla burst into the room like _____.

6. The whistle shrilled through the town like _____.

7. The box was as heavy as _____.

8. The math problem is as complicated as _____.

9. Manny drove the car like _____ through the city streets.

10. The knight was as determined as _____.

11. The man's voice was as loud as _____.

12. Hernando swims like _____.

13. I was as cold as _____ after the snowball fight.

14. She is as stubborn as _____.

15. The train whistle was as sad as _____.

Name _____ Date _____

Lady Liberty

The main idea of a paragraph is called the **topic**. One sentence usually tells what the topic is. That sentence is called the **topic sentence**. The topic sentence is often the first one in the paragraph. An editor must make sure that the topic sentence tells the main idea clearly.

Read the paragraph. Then answer the questions.

A sculptor named Bartholdi planned the statue. Another man, Gustave Eiffel, created the framework for the statue. The builders used iron for a framework, with a thin skin of copper on top of it. The statue took 15 years to make.

It was built in France but was taken apart to be shipped to America. It arrived here in 210 pieces! Today, the Statue of Liberty still stands in the harbor of New York. It is one of the most famous statues in the world.

Circle the right answer.

1. The topic sentence of the paragraph is missing. What is the main idea of the passage?

   a. touring New York City

   b. the history of the Statue of Liberty

   c. The centennial of the United States

   d. the Hudson River and its history

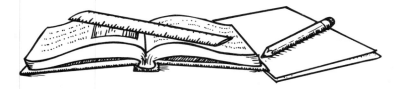

2. Choose the best topic sentence for the paragraph.

   a. The French are the best sculptors in the world, and two of the best were Eiffel and Bartholdi.

   b. When the United States turned 100 years old, France gave us an amazing gift—the Statue of Liberty.

   c. New York City is filled with amazing and awe-inspiring sights.

   d. Copper sculptures are very difficult to design and build.

3. Write your own topic sentence for the paragraph.

   _____

   _____

4. Choose two details that could be added to the paragraph.

   a. how the French raised the money to build the statue.

   b. why symbols of nations are so important

   c. how much it costs to visit the islands in New York's harbor

   d. the height of the Statue of Liberty

On Topic

The **topic sentence** tells the main idea of a paragraph. Often, the topic sentence comes first. The rest of the sentences tell more about that idea. Editors make sure that topic sentences are supported by the sentences that follow.

Match the topic sentence with the best supporting sentence below.

_____ 1. My dad says that people should try new experiences.

_____ 2. When I was small, my grandmother read *Alice in Wonderland* to me.

_____ 3. The new software program *Math Zap* makes math learning fun.

_____ 4. Even in the age of computers, handwriting is important.

_____ 5. I have never liked eggplant.

_____ 6. My parents think everyone should know how to play an instrument.

_____ 7. Telephones have made a big difference in people's lives.

_____ 8. I think that the Grand Canyon is the most inspiring natural wonder on Earth.

_____ 9. Our class must raise money if we are going to go on a class trip this year.

a. This book, written by Lewis Carroll has many strange characters.

b. Imagine not being able to call for help or to talk to a friend!

c. Everyone still needs to write something almost every day.

d. I am learning the piano, and my brother plays the clarinet.

e. Its huge cliffs, colored rocks, and deep valleys are amazingly beautiful.

f. That's why Dad took me whitewater rafting this summer.

g. Car washes, bake sales, and a school fair are all good ideas to meet this goal.

h. You won't believe how easy this program makes algebra and geometry!

i. That's why I was so surprised when I tasted my aunt's eggplant parmesan.

Deep Waters

A **topic sentence** tells the main idea in a paragraph. **Supporting sentences** give more details about the main idea. Editors make sure that each topic is supported by details. A paragraph often includes at least three key supporting sentences.

Read each topic sentence. Then circle three sentences that support each topic.

1. Since the year 565, many people near Loch Ness have told of seeing a strange animal in there.

    a. Loch Ness is deep enough to be the home for such a large animal.

    b. The monster has a long, snakelike neck and a small head.

    c. Another lake with a legend is Long Lake in Michigan.

    d. Most of those who have seen it say the Loch Ness Monster is dark and has a hump like a camel

    e. Camels are fascinating desert animals.

    f. Scotland is a mountainous and beautiful country.

2. In Tennessee, there is a large, beautiful lake inside a giant cave.

    a. Years ago, peopled named it "The Lost Sea."

    b. Tennessee also has beautiful mountains.

    c. In the 1800s, Native Americans used the cave as a hiding place.

    d. Caves often have strange rock formations.

    e. The cave of the Lost Sea was so large it was used as a dance hall.

    f. Caves can contain stalactites or stalagmites.

3. Another famous deep lake is Lake Huron.

    a. This Great Lake is the largest freshwater lake in the world.

    b. We went to Canada once to visit my cousins.

    c. Lake Huron is part of a shipping route that ends in Chicago.

    d. The northern end of the lake contains huge Manitoulin Island.

    e. Another one of the Great Lakes is Lake Superior.

    f. I love to go boating and fishing on freshwater lakes.

Beautiful Buildings

A topic sentence tells the main idea in a paragraph. Supporting sentences explain more about the main idea. Editors must make sure that each topic is supported by details. A paragraph often includes at least three key supporting sentences.

Read the paragraph. Then answer the questions about the details in the paragraph.

Mary Elizabeth Jane Colter was one of the few female architects in the United States before World War I. She graduated from the California School of Design and taught art to support her mother and sister. In the early 1900s, Colter was hired to design and decorate a building for Native American crafts at the Grand Canyon. She designed the building in a Hopi pueblo style. She wanted her building to look like it had been made long ago, so she used long beams and small branches in the ceiling. The building was made from red sandstone. Ladders connected its uneven rooftops. Hopi House, Hermit's Rest, Lookout Studio, Phantom Ranch, Watchtower, and Bright Angel Lodge are six Grand Canyon buildings that were designed by Mary Colter. In all of them, Colter created a lived-in look and a feeling of history. Four of the buildings are National Historic Landmarks.

1. According to the essay, how did Mary Colter make her crafts building look old?

    a. She made the walls look beaten-up and cracked.

    b. She put long beams and small branches in the ceiling, and the rooftops were uneven.

    c. She built the buildings at the Grand Canyon, and the canyon makes them look old.

    d. She did not finish the buildings so they would look empty.

2. What are the names of some of Mary Colter's buildings?

    a. Hope House, Hermit's Rest, and Phantom Ranch

    b. Hermit's Rest, Watchtower, and Bright Angle Lodge

    c. Hermit's Rest, Phantom Ranch, and Lookout Studio

    d. Watertower, Hermit's Rest, and Lookout Studio

3. Why do you think the author of the essay told us about the buildings becoming national landmarks?

    a. to show that Mary Colter's work was skilled and good

    b. to show that the buildings are very old and rundown

    c. to show that the California School of Design honored Mary Colter

    d. to show that Mary Colter was not an important architect

A Famous Writer

The **topic sentence** in a paragraph tells the main idea. **Supporting sentences** explain more about the main idea. Some supporting sentences give examples.

When writing more than one paragraph about a single subject, **the first paragraph** introduces the topic, just like the topic sentence in a paragraph. Supporting sentences develop, or tell more, about the topic. There is no concluding sentence because the writer has more ideas.

The next paragraph begins with a topic sentence that has a transition from the first paragraph to the next. **Transitions** help the reader follow the main idea. They show the order of events or how different ideas are connected. Supporting sentences develop the new idea.

The last paragraph concludes the writing. Like a concluding sentence, it should remind the reader of the topic or leave the reader with something to think about. This paragraph should contain the concluding sentence.

1. Read the three-paragraph essay. Then, choose which of the short, single paragraphs that follow it (a, b, or c) was expanded to create the essay.

Madeleine L'Engle was born on a snowy night in New York, in 1918. Her father was a writer. Her mother was a pianist. As Madeline grew up, visiting artists were always in her home. When she was 12, her family moved to Europe, where Madeleine went to a boarding school. She returned to America to attend Smith College.

Her first book, called *A Small Rain*, was published in 1945. It is a story about a girl at boarding school who escapes her worries by playing the piano. Madeleine continued to write and publish different types of books. *A Wrinkle in Time*, L'Engle's most famous book, was rejected by 26 publishers. Finally, one publishing company took a chance and published her book. One year later, this imaginative book won the Newbery Award.

Writing has been a lifelong passion for Madeleine. She began writing when she could first hold a pencil. She has never stopped, and that is a benefit for those who love her books.

a. Many authors write interesting science fiction and fantasy stories. One of these is Madeleine L'Engle. Another good author is Garth Nix. Philip Pullman wrote a famous fantasy trilogy.

b. The Newbery Award is the most important award in children's literature. One year, a biography of Abraham Lincoln by Russell Freedman won. Another year, it was the science fiction novel *A Wrinkle in Time* by Madeleine L'Engle. Louis Sachar's novel *Holes*, set in a boys' detention center, also won the award.

c. Madeleine L'Engle was born in 1918. She published her first novel, *A Small Rain*, in 1945. Writing has been her lifelong passion. That passion was well rewarded when her book *A Wrinkle in Time* won the Newbery Award in 1963.

A Famous Writer (cont.)

Reread the three-paragraph essay about Madeleine L'Engle on page 34. Then answer the questions below about the supporting details in the essay.

2. According to the essay, how does Madeleine feel about writing?

   a. She started writing at a very young age but does not write today.

   b. She did not enjoy writing about boarding schools and soon quit. However, she loves writing science fiction books.

   c. She feels that writing is something she does very well. After all, she won the Newbery Award.

   d. Writing has been her lifelong passion.

3. Why do you think the author of the essay told about Madeleine's parents?

   a. They were not kind to her, and that's why she started writing.

   b. They were involved in creative work themselves, and that might be how Madeleine got interested in writing.

   c. Her father was a pianist, so the family was probably poor.

   d. Later on in her life, Madeleine wrote *A Wrinkle in Time*, a book about music.

4. Why do you think the author of the essay told about Madeleine's time in boarding school?

   a. Her first book was about a girl in a boarding school, and she probably got the idea for it because of her own time in school.

   b. The author wanted to show that Madeleine had a good education, and that's why she is a good writer.

   c. She went to school in Europe and later went back there to live again.

   d. She probably daydreamed a lot in school and then became a writer after that.

Paragraph Power

A **paragraph** is a group of sentences that tells the reader about one main idea.

This is a paragraph:

　　The **topic sentence** tells the main idea of the paragraph. Often, the topic sentence comes first. The rest of the sentences tell more about the idea. These are called **supporting sentences**. All of the sentences in a paragraph describe one main idea. The first line of the paragraph is **indented**, which means it is moved in from the left side.

Remember that paragraphs have a formula:

　　The first line is indented.

　　The first sentence is usually the topic sentence.

　　The other sentences support the topic sentence with details

Read each paragraph. Then choose the number of the sentence that does not belong in the paragraph.

1.　(1) Choosing a vacation place is hard. (2) Beaches offer swimming, body surfing, and sandcastle building during a vacation. (3) Mountains offer kayaking, hiking, and wildlife watching. (4) Mountain animals have to be able to stand hard winters with lots of snow. (5) It can be a difficult choice!

　　a.　sentence 2　　　　　　　　　　c.　sentence 4

　　b.　sentence 3　　　　　　　　　　d.　sentence 5

2.　(1) Have you ever received a thank-you note? (2) What a wonderful feeling to know that someone appreciates something you did or a gift you gave! (3) One great gift is new computer software, especially a game. (4) But many people are not certain how to say "thank you" in written form. (5) Writing a thank-you note is actually quite simple—when you know the secrets, of course!

　　a.　sentence 2　　　　　　　　　　c.　sentence 4

　　b.　sentence 3　　　　　　　　　　d.　sentence 5

3.　(1) The margay is an endangered species that lives in rain forests.(2) These nocturnal animals live almost their whole lives in the high canopy of trees. (3) Other rain-forest animals are lizards, panthers, and monkeys. (4) Their hind legs are able to turn all the way around, which allows them to climb up and down trees face first, like squirrels.

　　a.　sentence 1　　　　　　　　　　c.　sentence 3

　　b.　sentence 2　　　　　　　　　　d.　sentence 4

A Mysterious Island

A paragraph is a group of sentences that tells the reader about the main idea. If sentences do not support the main idea, they do not belong in the paragraph. The editor must take them out. The editor must also know when a new paragraph starts.

This is the mark to take out a sentence that does not belong: _ℓ_ .

This is the mark to show the start of a new paragraph: ⊤P.

Use proofreading marks to edit the paragraphs. Show which sentences do not belong and where new paragraphs start, including the first paragraph.

On Easter Sunday in 1722, Jacob Roggevan and his crew landed on Easter Island. The Dutch have always been famous for their seagoing adventures. The astonished crew found dozens of huge stone figures standing on long stone platforms. Some of the statues were 40 feet tall. They had expressionless faces without eyes. There were also extinct volcanoes on the island. Big stone cylinders were placed on their heads. The mystery of these statues was not solved during Roggevan's lifetime. Archaeologists now believe that three different cultures had lived on Easter Island. The first group, from about A.D. 400, were people who made small stone sculptures. The second group, who lived centuries later, tore down the small statues and used them to build platforms for temples. These were also the artists who carved the enormous heads. The last group invaded the island in 1670. They were cannibals. They destroyed the culture that had created the temples and had lived on the island peacefully. Cannibals also lived at that time in Indonesia. Today, Easter Island is governed by Chile. Other countries in South America include Paraguay and Peru. Almost the entire population of the island lives in the village of Hanga Roa, on the west coast of this mysterious island.

◆◆◆◆◆◆◆◆◆◆◆◆◆◆◆◆◆◆◆◆◆◆◆◆◆◆◆◆◆◆◆◆◆◆◆◆

Fire!

Paragraphs are made up of sentences that all support the main idea. But in stories, there are other reasons to end one paragraph and start another. When a different character speaks, the editor must begin a new paragraph.

This is the mark to show the beginning of a new paragraph: ₸.

◆◆◆◆◆◆◆◆◆◆◆◆◆◆◆◆◆◆◆◆◆◆◆◆◆◆◆◆◆◆◆◆◆◆◆◆

Use the paragraph mark to show where new paragraphs start in this story.

"Quiet down, students. Please go to your desks," Mr. Chan said to the class. He waited for everyone to get settled. "Now, please take out your writing journals. Today, we will be learning about inferencing." "Is that like conferencing?" Daphne asked eagerly. The students often had conferences to talk about their stories. Daphne had just finished a good story. "No," answered Mr. Chan. "But that's a good guess. In fact, that is what inferencing is—a guess based on what you already know. Daphne saw that we were using our journals. She made an inference that we would be doing something with writing. Great inference, Daphne!" Just then, a loud noise rang through the room. "It must be a fire drill," said Stephen to Daphne. The students lined up and walked single file to the playground door. "Please stay together," said Mr. Chan. "I will go talk to the principal and see what is happening." The students stood quietly until they saw a large red truck pull up alongside the school. "Look!" cried Melissa. "It's the fire truck!" said Stephen. The students began talking and pointing. Then Keisha turned around. "Look at the roof! There's smoke!" she called to the others. "Don't worry," said Mr. Chan, coming back to the group. "Everyone is safe. There was a small fire in the cafeteria kitchen. Something was left in the oven too long and it caught on fire. But I'm going to make an inference right now. I infer that we may be eating lunch in our room today instead of in the cafeteria!"

The Amazing Mozart

The **topic sentence** in a paragraph tells the main idea. Supporting sentences explain more about the main idea. One job of an editor is to make sure that the sentences are written in an order that makes sense.

The story below is mixed up. Read all the sentences first. On the line, write a number 1 to show which sentence should come first. Number the other sentences to show their correct order. Underline the topic sentences of the paragraphs. (Hint: There are three paragraphs.)

_____ Mozart's father toured with his son, who played for kings and queens at courts throughout Europe.

_____ Toward the end of his life, Mozart began working on a piece called "Requiem."

_____ Mozart wrote many types of music: operas, symphonies, serenades, and church music.

_____ A *requiem* is a piece of music that is played at funerals.

_____ Wolfgang Amadeus Mozart was born in 1756 in Austria.

_____ Although his life was short, Mozart's music was inspiring and still inspires us today.

_____ Sadly, Mozart was ill at the time he began writing this funeral piece.

_____ To support his wife, he began selling the music he had written.

_____ When he was just three years old, he learned to play the harpsichord.

_____ When Mozart became an adult, he moved to Vienna and married.

_____ He died on December 5, 1791, at the age of 35.

_____ The composer also made money by giving music lessons and performing concerts.

_____ The child Mozart astonished these royal listeners with his musical genius.

Write another sentence that could be a part of this story.

_____

Name

Date

Walking a Thin Line

A **paragraph** is a group of sentences that tells the reader about one main idea. Editors must know where one paragraph ends and another starts. They also need to check that paragraphs are written in an order that makes sense.

Read Jacob's report about an athlete named Charles Blondin. In the blanks, number the paragraphs to show their correct order.

_____ It was not his acrobatics as a child that astonished the world but what Blondin did later in his life. The French acrobat is most famous for his performances over Niagara Falls, which began in 1859. He stretched a rope 1,100 feet (336 m) from one side of the falls to the other. To the amazement of the crowd, Charles Blondin crossed the falls on that thin rope. How could anyone top such a feat?

_____ Do you know the name Charles Blondin? Have you heard of Niagara Falls? Charles Blondin was famous in his day for his amazing performances at this natural wonder.

_____ Today, most people do not know the name of Charles Blondin. But in his own time, he made history. The Little Wonder of France became a big name around the world.

_____ The answer was that Charles Blondin topped his own performance at least four more times! He later crossed Niagara Falls blindfolded, and then he pushed a wheelbarrow across the tightrope. During another performance, he carried a small stove. He stopped halfway across the falls to cook and eat an omelet.

_____ Born in Saint-Omer, France, this acrobat's real name was Jean-Francois Gravelet. He became known as the Little Wonder early in his life. At the age of six, he was already performing daring feats.

Strong Arguments

A **paragraph** is a group of sentences that tells the reader about one main idea. It has a topic sentence, supporting sentences, and a concluding sentence. An editor must make sure that the details in the paragraph support the topic sentence. One type of paragraph in which this is very important is when a writer is expressing an opinion.

Read each opinion. Then circle the reason that best supports each opinion.

1. Bike riders should wear helmets.

Reasons:
     a. Helmets look cool and come in lots of colors.
     b. A helmet can save your life if you are in an accident.
     c. Helmets are hot and uncomfortable to wear.

2. The school year should be longer.

Reasons:
     a. The longer the time we have to learn, the smarter we will be.
     b. Summer vacations are boring.
     c. There are too many snow days during the winter.

If the reasons that support an opinion are not good, the editor may have to rewrite them. Fill in the line to finish the topic sentence. Then write three reasons that support the topic sentence.

3. _____ is the best show on TV.
    (Fill in your favorite show.)

Reasons:
     a. _____
     b. _____
     c. _____

4. _____ is the hardest subject in school for me.
    (Fill in your choice.)

Reasons:
     a. _____
     b. _____
     c. _____

Tons of Trash

A **paragraph** is a group of sentences that tells about one main idea.
Editors must know where one paragraph ends and another starts. Editors
use this mark to show the start of a new paragraph: ¶.
They use other proofreading marks to fix other mistakes in the paragraphs.

Read this story. Use proofreading marks to fix the mistakes. Use the paragraph mark to show
where each new paragraph begins.

Did you know that the average american throws away about five ponds of trash a day? That's over

half a Ton a year! Where does it go? for years we piled it up in *landfills*, a nise name for dumps.

Mountains of trash and garbage where covered with dirt or plastic. these heaps were left to rot.

Unfortunately, that didnt happen. For garbage to decae, there must be enough air and water for

bacteria to grow. The bactera didn't grow inside the dumps covered heaps. *Garbologists*, garbage

scientists from the University of arizona, dug into an old landfill. What they discovered surprized

them. Thay found 50-year-old newspapers they could still read! The papers helped them date the

layers of trash. in the layers, they also found Corn on the cob, green grass clippings, and a whole

hot dog! Someday, we may be able to figure out how to build a landfill that realy rots. But Earths

running out of space for our trash. The best way to solve our trash problem is to make less trash!

Heres how: Recicle. Buy things made from or recycled materials. complain to companies that use

too much paper or plastic. help save Earth before its just one big garbage dump!

Name _____ Date _____

Talking About Topics

A paragraph is a group of sentences that tells about one main idea. Editors look at many things when they proofread paragraphs. One thing they do is make sure the paragraph's sentences work together. Editors must know the topic and check that it is supported by details.

Read the paragraph. Choose the best topic sentence.

1.   They sent up a rooster, a sheep, and a duck on this first flight. The landmark event took place in 1783, in Paris. King Louis XVI and Marie Antoinette watched the balloon sail into the sky.
   a. The first person to fly was Pilatre de Rozier.
   b. The Montgolfier brothers were the first people to send up a hot-air balloon.
   c. People have always dreamed of flying.
   d. The French Revolution was only a few years away.

Circle the letter of the answer that best supports each topic sentence.

2. Los Angeles, California, is a favorite spot for vacations.
   a. California lies along the San Andreas Fault.
   b. People love to see the homes of movie stars and go to the beaches.
   c. San Francisco is the home of the famous Golden Gate Bridge.

3. Native Americans used to tell stories about the natural world.
   a. The Greeks had legends about the gods on Mount Olympus.
   b. Thunder and lightning also occurred in ancient times.
   c. The Cherokees, for example, have a legend about how fire came to Earth.

4. Japanese children go to school six days a week.
   a. Japan holds a cherry blossom festival every spring.
   b. Another country in Asia is Thailand.
   c. If American students went to school on Saturdays, it would give them more time to learn their lessons, as the Japanese do.

5. Write a supporting sentence for this topic sentence: Pizza is the nation's favorite food.

_____

_____

         0-7424-2755-2 *Proofreading & Editing*

Titles Are Telling

An editor must know the reason, or **purpose**, for writing. He or she must also know who the readers, or **audience**, will be. The title of a piece of writing tells a lot about the purpose and the audience.

Circle the letter of the best title for each audience and purpose.

1. **Audience**: your teacher and classmates

   Purpose: give a report about your winter vacation
   a. Why I Hate Winter
   b. My Skiing Vacation
   c. How Snow Is Formed

2. **Audience**: the math club

   Purpose: tell about the history of math discoveries
   a. Algebra and You
   b. My Struggle With Math
   c. Great Moments in Math History

3. **Audience**: a younger class

   Purpose: tell about safety tips
   a. My First-Grade Teacher
   b. Why Safety Counts
   c. First-Grade Math Lessons

4. **Audience**: a class newsletter

   Purpose: say goodbye to a teacher who is leaving
   a. Mr. Strengholt's Summer Vacation
   b. Mr. Strengholt's Life as a Student
   c. We'll Miss You, Mr. Strengholt!

Now write titles for these pieces.

5. **Audience**: your teacher and classmates

   Purpose: tell a story about your most memorable moment

   _____

6. **Audience**: your grandparents

   Purpose: an essay about a trip you took with them

   _____

The Right Topics

Before starting to proofread, it is important that an editor know the audience for a piece. The **audience** means the people who will be reading the piece of writing. An editor makes sure that the topic is written in a way that will interest the audience.

Circle the letter of the right answer to each question.

1. A book called *Emergency Rules for Schools* would be of interest to—
   a. homeowners.
   b. elementary school principals.
   c. parents.
   d. toddlers.

2. Choose the audience most interested in a book about how parents can help students with easy ways to learn algebra.
   a. newborn babies
   b. first graders
   c. cafeteria workers
   d. parents of students

3. The audience most interested in a speech called *Your Ferret and You* would be—
   a. kindergartners.
   b. pet owners.
   c. joggers.
   d. none of the these

4. Choose the audience who would be most interested in a book titled *The Best Books for All Ages.*
   a. third graders
   b. fifth graders
   c. teenagers
   d. all of these

5. Javonte wants to write a letter to the newspaper about how people need to slow down on his street. Choose the best first sentence.

   a. Learning to drive is important and also difficult.

   b. Alten Avenue has lots of children and too many fast cars.

   c. Driving fast can be fun.

6. Shaya is writing a story about her family's cabin at a lake. Choose the best first sentence.

   a. Summer vacations are important breaks for students.

   b. Our little house is not on the prairie but on Loon Lake.

   c. Log cabins have a long and interesting history.

A Sense of Purpose

An editor must know the reason, or **purpose**, for writing. She or he must also know who the readers, or **audience**, will be. If the writing doesn't match the audience, the editor has to think of ways to make it fit better.

Match each topic sentence to the right audience and purpose.

_____1. When you are assigning values in probability, start with zero—that's an event that will never happen.

_____2. My kitten, Scratch, is the bravest animal I have ever met.

_____3. If you like the *Harry Potter* books, you should also read the novels by Philip Pullman.

_____4. Dear Diary: Today was one of the greatest days of my life.

_____5. There are about 900 known species of bats.

_____6. Sir Isaac Newton was one of the most important scientists who ever lived.

a. **Audience**: your teacher and classmates
   Purpose: write a report about an animal family

b. **Audience**: your teacher and classmates
   Purpose: report on a math principle

c. **Audience**: the book club
   Purpose: report on a book you want others to read

d. **Audience**: yourself
   Purpose: record your life in a diary

e. **Audience**: your teacher and classmates
   Purpose: give a speech about a pet

f. **Audience**: the science club newsletter
   Purpose: write about a famous scientist

Hear, Hear!

The editor must know who the **audience** will be before editing. Sometimes it is easier to identify the audience and fit the topic to the audience when the piece of writing is a speech.

Circle the letter that shows the audience to whom each speech was given.

1. Did you see a dinosaur on your way to school today? Of course not! That's because dinosaurs lived long, long ago. We can see models of them in museums. Some of the models even move, but they're not alive. Dinosaurs have been extinct, or no longer on Earth, for millions of years.

   a. a group of senior citizens

   b. a college science class

   c. a kindergarten class

   d. a group of science teachers

2. Since there were no cameras in prehistoric times, there are no old photos of dinosaurs. So early scientists used if-then thinking to decide what colors to put on museum models: "If dinosaurs were lizardlike, then they probably looked a lot like today's lizards. And if today's lizards are gray, brown, or green, then dinosaurs were probably the same colors." That's why most dinosaur models are the same colors as today's lizards.

   a. visitors to a natural history museum

   b. a meeting of the math club

   c. a pep rally for the school football team

   d. a class reunion dinner party

3. When telling young people about prehistoric animals, stress that *prehistoric* means "before written records." Remind them that no one knows exactly why dinosaurs are extinct because no one was there to witness it. But scientists do have theories. Most relate to changes in Earth's climate after a gigantic meteorite crashed into Earth's surface. One interesting theory is that increasingly hot weather caused more male than female dinosaurs to develop. So, dinosaurs became extinct because there were no females to increase their population!

   a. a fifth grade class

   b. visitors at a new mall

   c. science teachers

   d. a parent-teacher meeting

The Best Words

When you know your audience and your topics, you can check **vocabulary**. Some words that are good to use in a letter to a friend are not the words you want to use in your report for school. Sometimes writers use the wrong word for a certain topic. An editor must choose words that will help the audience understand the writing.

Circle the best word to use in the piece of writing for each audience and purpose.

1. **Audience**: your teacher and classmates

   Purpose: a report about animal habitats

   a. basement

   b. burrow

   c. Mars

2. **Audience**: the hiking club

   Purpose: tell about a nature hike

   a. breakthrough

   b. kilometers

   c. vacation

3. **Audience**: a younger class

   Purpose: a speech about your favorite picture book

   a. scientific

   b. logical

   c. funny

4. **Audience**: a class newsletter

   Purpose: write about a field trip

   a. empty

   b. educational

   c. clever

5. **Audience**: toy buyers

   Purpose: an ad about a new toy

   a. unbreakable

   b. unhappy

   c. unimaginative

6. **Audience**: your aunt and uncle

   Purpose: thank them for a gift

   a. tiny

   b. generous

   c. breakthrough

7. **Audience**: the school community

   Purpose: announce a new safety rule

   a. cute

   b. quiet

   c. important

          0-7424-2755-2 *Proofreading & Editing*

The Best Words (cont.)

Cross out the word that does not belong in each sentence. Use this mark: ℓ. Then write a word on the line to replace the one you have taken out of the sentence.

8. Bats can't walk or run because their feet aren't cute or strong.

    _____

9. Tristan and Jake went to the movies and bought hot, sour popcorn.

    _____

10. The Underground Railroad was a system made up of faint, brave people who helped runaway slaves escape to freedom.

    _____

11. Henry Hudson searched the Hudson River and Hudson Bay.

    _____

12. Tabitha is my best friend; she is smart, funny, and papery.

    _____

13. Find the answer to this amusing equation; be sure to show your work.

    _____

Write a sentence that uses these words: my state, famous, landmark

14. _____

    _____

15. Use proofreading marks to edit the incorrect words in the beginning of this report. Add new words only if the sentences need them in order to be clear.

    Elephants are peaceful and small animals. They live in social groups similar to families. There is one female elephant, called the matriarch, that leads the tribe. As one of the largest land birds in the world, African elephants have few predators. In fact, one of the fewest dangers to elephants in past years has not been from other animals but from humans. Hunters hate their ivory tusks.

Word Choices

When you know your audience and your topics, you must check **vocabulary**. Sometimes writers choose words that don't belong in a piece of writing. Sometimes writers use the wrong word. An editor chooses words that will help the audience understand the writing.

Read each paragraph. Then choose the word that could also be used in the paragraph.

1.   My family helps at the hospital every Labor Day. This holiday is supposed to be one for all workers, but hospital workers must stay on the job. Each one of us in the family takes a job so that one of the health-care workers can enjoy the day with her or his family.
   a. volunteer
   b. review
   c. edit

2.   Mr. Stawski is our teacher. He is also a writer. He's published articles in magazines for students our age. His stories are interesting and funny. He's always got new ideas for more writing!
   a. fair
   b. creative
   c. angry

3.   Baseball is an important part of American culture and history. The World Series is the most exciting sports event of the year. It determines the national champion in America's favorite pastime.
   a. firefighter
   b. home run
   c. craft

4.   Who invented television? It was not just one inventor. In the 1800s, an Italian inventor named Marconi found how to send signals through the air. Later, a young American named Philo Farnsworth began experiments. He had an idea to send pictures, as well as sound, through the air. At about the same time, a scientist named Zworykin invented a tube that could receive and show pictures.
   a. discovered
   b. wrote
   c. baked

A World of Ice

Sometimes writers choose words that don't belong in a piece of writing. Sometimes they use the wrong word. An editor takes out words that don't fit and chooses words that will help the audience understand the writing.

1. Read the paragraph. Use this mark to take out words that don't belong: ℓ . Write a new word above the deleted word to replace the one that you take out.

Antarctica is the continent above the South Pole. It contains 90 percent of the world's ice. Antarctica is the coldest and most popular region on Earth. It covers over five million square miles. Much of the land is swimming under snow and ice that is more than a mile thick.

The interior of Antartica is hot and lifeless. The only animal life on this continent is found on the coastline or in the sea. Penguins, seals, whales, and other fish and birds live in or close to the coastal waters. These people find their food in the sea.

For centuries, the town was unexplored. In 1911, Roald Amundsen traveled to the South Pole. In 1928, Commander Richard Byrd led a forgotten expedition to the Pole. The whole world heard of his exploration. He helped to set up scientific bases on other trips to this silly continent.

Circle the letter of the correct answer to each question.

2. In the first paragraph, which word might also fit?

   a. desolate

   b. friendly

   c. wasteful

3. In the second paragraph, which phrase would also fit?

   a. knowledgeable people

   b. harsh environment

   c. careful planning

4. In the third paragraph, which sentence would also fit?

   a. Amundsen and Byrd were both popular leaders.

   b. Amundsen and Byrd were brave explorers.

   c. Amundsen and Byrd were from two different countries.

It Fits

Editors must make sure that **titles** and **subheads** fit the piece of writing. A title should either clearly tell what a piece of writing is about or it should make a reader curious to find out more. If a title or subhead doesn't fit, the editor may change it.

Read each opening paragraph. Choose the best title for the whole selection, based on the part that you have read.

1.   Everyone should collect stamps. It is fun, and it is also a hobby that can earn you money. A stamp that my uncle bought ten years ago for twenty cents just sold for thirty dollars.
   a. "Stamp Collecting for Fun and Profit"
   b. "My Uncle, the Stamp Collector"
   c. "Stamps: Mysterious Art Forms"

2.   The little brown bat is the most common bat in North America. This bat is just three-and-a-half inches long, and it weighs about one-half ounce. It spends its day in caves, hollow trees, attics, or under roofs. During the winter, the little brown bat hibernates in a cave.
   a. "The Life and Times of Brownie Bat"
   b. "North American Bats"
   c. "The Little Brown Bat"

3.   Columbus went to the New World. Henry Hudson explored the Hudson River Valley. And my family and I ventured into Sea World one hot, humid day in August. Our encounter with another world had begun.
   a. "Explorers of North America"
   b. "Columbus, Hudson, and Me"
   c. "Exploring New Continents"

4.   Ancient Rome was a powerful civilization that began almost 3,000 years ago. The Romans wore clothing that was simple and comfortable, but they also had luxuries such as indoor plumbing. They were famous for their many festivals and special events. They loved to feast and celebrate.
   a. "The Luxury-Loving Romans"
   b. "The Rise and Fall of the Roman Empire"
   c. "The History of Roman Government"

◆◆◆◆◆◆◆◆◆◆◆◆◆◆◆◆◆◆◆◆◆◆◆◆◆◆◆◆◆◆◆

It Fits (cont.)

Editors look at both **titles** and **subheads** when they edit. Not all types of writing have subheads, but reports often do. Usually, a report will start with a title. At the first break in the report, the writer uses the first subhead. Other subheads show where the information in the report changes. The editor makes sure that the title and the subheads are different and that each subhead lets the reader know what the next section of the report is about.

◆◆◆◆◆◆◆◆◆◆◆◆◆◆◆◆◆◆◆◆◆◆◆◆◆◆◆◆◆◆◆

Read the report. Then write a title or subhead for each numbered section. Remember, the first blank is for the title for the whole report, not just the first section.

5. _____

The first modern-day computer in the U. S. was ENIAC. Built at the University of Pennsylvania in 1945, ENIAC weighed about thirty tons. It had thousands of electrical switches, called vacuum tubes, to do mathematical calculations.

6. _____

ENIAC was useful but had no "memory" for storing data. That made reusing the information difficult. Soon scientists developed computers with memory. The first ones still filled entire rooms. They weren't very fast, but they could be programmed to work through the night while the humans slept.

7. _____

Everything changed in 1947 when the transistor was invented. It weighed a hundred times less than a vacuum tube. It broke down far less frequently and was much faster. Then another breakthrough happened in 1971. The microchip was created. It could run an entire computer. One microchip about the size of a penny can hold more than 200,000 transistors! This date marked the birth of the computer as we know it today.

Write an answer to each question.

8. What information do you think will be in the next paragraph of this report?

_____

_____

9. Write a subhead for the next section as you imagine it.

_____

10. If this report was one article in a book of articles about changes in technology, what would be a good title for the book?

_____

Summing It Up

A **summary** tells the main points of a longer piece of writing. It tells main ideas of the original but not all of the details. Sometimes editors must read and edit summaries. Sometimes, an editor will write a summary of a longer piece.

Read these selections. Underline the topic sentence or main idea of each paragraph.

1.   People have always looked to the heavens for clues to the world around them. A buffalo-shaped cloud might tell an ancient hunter when to hunt. Sailors watched clouds to predict the weather. Even the constellations told people when seasons would change. Clouds, stars, sun, and moon have all shared their secrets with humankind.

2.   Can a human run faster than a horse? Several track runners have proven their super speed by racing 50 meters against horses. A human can accelerate more quickly than a horse. The horse is slower to start but has a much higher maximum speed. As a result, if the race is short enough, a human can cross the finish line before a horse!

Read the following paragraphs. Choose the best summary.

3   Carlos asked Kori, the smart girl who sat next to him, if she would help him pass tomorrow's history test. Carlos planned to move his desk closer to see her answers. Korri had a different plan. After school, she met with Carlos and they studied together all evening. Carlos found that by studying, he knew the correct answers.

   a. Carlos planned to copy test answers from Kori.

   b. Carlos and Kori sat next to one another in history.

   c. Carlos did not like to study.

   d. Kori helped Carlos study to pass his history test.

4.   Amelia rested her chin in her hand, her elbow on the windowsill, and her eyes on the gloomy distance. She sighed as she watched the sheets of rain crashing down from the dark, heavy skies. Her forehead slumped forward and pressed against the cold glass, knocking the cap from her head. She looked down at the cap, lying next to her bat and mitt, and sighed again.

   a. Amelia felt excited about the large storm.

   b. Friends of Amelia's were coming to visit, but she could not see them through the rain.

   c. Amelia wanted to play baseball but could not, due to the storm.

   d. Amelia enjoyed watching for lightning outside her cold window.

Can You Paraphrase?

To **paraphrase** means to restate something in different words. If editors are working with an author's paraphrasing of another source, they must make sure that the idea has been restated correctly.

Read each part of the report about George Washington Carver. Choose the sentence that best paraphrases the paragraph.

1.   George Washington Carver was born in Missouri in 1864. He was born a slave. As a child he became really interested in plants. People even called him "the plant doctor." When he was 12, he went away to school. He got a job to pay his way and lived with families who would take him in. By 1896, he had earned two college degrees. He became a teacher at the Tuskegee Institute in Alabama.

   a. The author tells how George Washington Carver was born in slavery in Missouri. From the time Carver was a young child, he was very interested in plants. At 12, he went to school and worked to pay for his schooling. He earned two college degrees and became a teacher at the Tuskegee Institute.

   b. The author tells about George Washington Carver as a child. Carver was born in 1864. People called him "the plant doctor." When he was 12, he started school. Eventually, he earned two college degrees. Then he got a job to pay back the money for his schooling.

2.   Carver is best known for his work in agriculture. To help farmers, he experimented to develop new products made from peanuts and sweet potatoes, plants that would enrich the soil. From peanuts, he made more than 300 new products, including coffee, cheese, milk, ink, flour, and soap. He also made more than 100 new products from sweet potatoes, including molasses, flour, rubber, and glue. For his work, Carver received many honors. He was proud of the work he did to help farmers.

   a. The author tells about Carver's experiments with plants. Carver invented many products, such as ink and soap. He also discovered how to make molasses. For these inventions, Carver received medals and honors.

   b. The author tells how Carver decided to help farmers by finding new ways to make products from peanuts and sweet potatoes. He experimented with the plants. He discovered more than 300 new ways to use peanuts and more than 100 ways to use sweet potatoes. He was awarded many honors because of his work.

Go to the Source!

When you proofread, sometimes you must check **sources**. These are the places where the writer found information. An editor makes sure that facts, dates, and other information in the piece of writing are correct. The sources help the editor make sure that everything in the writing is correct.

Choose which source would help you the most to proofread and check each piece of writing.

1. a report about a new building in your town

    a. a newspaper article about the building

    b. a dictionary

    c. a magazine article about architecture

    d. volume B of the encyclopedia

2. an article about Parents' Night at your school

    a. an outline about parenting

    b. volume P of the encyclopedia

    c. an interview with the author's parents about the event

    d. a report about your school's budget

3. a book report

    a. a history of bookbinding

    b. a story about the same topic

    c. the library catalog listing of the book

    d. a story about a student who writes a book report

4. the science club newsletter

    a. notes about new science club events

    b. a story about kids doing an experiment

    c. volume S of the encyclopedia

    d. a report about starting clubs at school

5. What sources could you use to help you edit a report about modern explorers?

    _____

    _____

6. What sources could you use to help you edit a short story about a family that moves to Ecuador?

    _____

    _____

Runaway Buffalo

When you look at a piece of writing, sometimes you must check **sources**. These are the places where the writer found information. An editor makes sure that facts, dates, and other details in the piece of writing are correct. The sources help the editor make sure that everything in the writing is correct.

Here is a newspaper article. Juana used this article to write her report, below.

Yellowstone Lake, WY—Two teens discovered a buffalo on tiny Stephenson Island yesterday. Kim Wilson and Ang Chen of Brookline, MA, had paddled a canoe out to the island to go hiking. They saw the buffalo while walking on the island.

"We had been on the island for about a half hour. We knew that we couldn't go to the south side of the island. There are eagles nesting there. We walked through the meadow in the center of the island. We had no idea a buffalo was there, or we wouldn't have gone," said Kim. Ang added that the pair walked slowly back to their canoe and left immediately.

During the winter months, rangers had seen the buffalo walk across the ice to the island. They had kept tracking it after that, but they had not seen it for more than three months. They thought it was no longer on the island. Until further notice, the island is off limits to tourists.

Here is Juana's report. Underline any fact that does not match the information in the article.

Sometimes wild animals are in places where you least expect them. That's what happened to

Kim Wilson and Ang Chan of Brookline. While on a trip to Wyoming, the two teens visited

Stephenson Island. They had rowed to the island to go hiking. Because they did not want to bother

some eagles that were nesting on the north side of the island, they walked through the center of the

island instead. That's when they saw the buffalo. Park rangers had no idea that the buffalo had

gone to the island. The two teens escaped by swimming back to shore. They shared their story in

the newspaper last week.

A Report About George

An editor makes sure that facts, dates, and other details in the piece of writing are right. The sources help the editor do this. Sometimes the editor must check two sources. The sources may have different information.

Keisha is writing a report about George Washington. She has found a timeline of the major events in his life. She also made an outline that she wrote while she was reading books about Washington. Read the timeline and her outline. Then answer the questions on page 59.

Source 1: Timeline

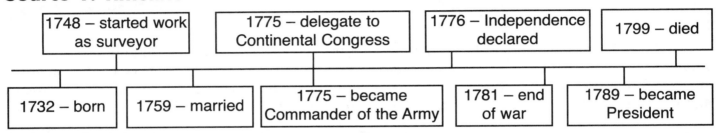

| 1748 – started work as surveyor | 1775 – delegate to Continental Congress | 1776 – Independence declared | 1799 – died |

| 1732 – born | 1759 – married | 1775 – became Commander of the Army | 1781 – end of war | 1789 – became President |

Source 2: Outline from Notes by Keisha Morehouse

I.   WASHINGTON'S CHILDHOOD
   A.   Born 1732 in Westmoreland County, Virginia
   B.   Father dies in 1743
   C.   Student at the Henry Williams School
      1.   Good at math
      2.   Liked mapmaking

II. WASHINGTON AS A SURVEYOR
   A.   Surveyed land beyond the Blue Ridge Mountains
   B.   Appointed surveyor of Culpepper County at age 17

III. WASHINGTON'S MILITARY CAREER
   A.   Served in the French and Indian War
      1.   Became a lieutenant colonel
      2.   Had two horses shot from under him
   B.   Revolutionary War
      1.   Elected Commander of the Army at the Second Continental Congress
      2.   Played a key part in winning the Revolutionary War

IV. SERVED AT CONSTITUTIONAL CONVENTION OF 1787

V.   PRESIDENCY FROM 1789 TO 1797
   A.   Elected unanimously
   B.   As first President, helped create the office

A Report About George (cont.)

Use the sources on page 58 to check the information in Keisha's report. Underline any phrase or sentence that has information that is not the same as information in the sources. Keisha also put information in the report from other sources.

George Washington probably thought he would be a farmer all his life. He was born in 1733. His father died when he was 11 years old. When Washington went to school, he found he liked math and mapmaking. So the job of surveyor, a person who measures land for maps and deeds, was perfect for him. When he was just 17 years old, he was made the surveyor for Westmoreland County, Virginia. He traveled beyond the Blue Ridge Mountains to survey land for maps.

Later, Washington served in the French and Indian War. He survived having a horse shot out from underneath him. But even though he was promoted, Washington was not ready to be a lieutenant colonel. After making a terrible mistake during a frontier campaign, he left the army. He married Martha Custis in 1759 and settled down to farm.

But when the Revolutionary War started, Washington was ready to serve. He was made Commander of the Army in 1776. The war was long and difficult. It lasted until 1781. Washington's plans for battles and his leadership made a big difference in the success of the war.

After the Constitutional Convention in 1789, Washington became the country's first President. He showed great leadership in this important role. After leaving office, Washington retired in 1799.

Write short answers to the questions.

1. Where do you think Keisha found the name of President Washington's wife?

   _____

2. Where would Keisha have found the information about Washington's French and Indian War experience?

   _____

3. What source did Keisha use to find the meaning of the word *surveyor*?

   _____

4. From your own knowledge about Washington, what is one other detail that Keisha could have included in her report?

   _____

   _____

Eyewitness Reports

An editor must make sure that facts, dates, and other details in the piece of writing are correct. The sources help the editor do that. Sometimes the editor has to check three sources. The sources may have different information.

At the mall, shoppers were surprised to see a visitor from outer space! Read the reports of two shoppers and the mall manager. Then read the newspaper article on page 61.

Source 1: Shopper Justina Reginald

I am Justina Reginald. I was walking to the shoe store when I saw an alien from outer space! He was waving his arms at a group of workers who were building something in the center of the mall. I think it was some kind of bandstand. The alien was dressed completely in white. His face was dark and shiny, like a mirror. He didn't have any eyes! It was scary. Every mother in the place was pulling her children to the nearest exit. People were running everywhere; all you could hear were pounding feet. The alien ran away from the shoppers and toward one of the stores. It was about 3 o'clock. I forgot all about shoe shopping. I just got out of there fast!

Source 2: Shopper Erin Thompson

My name is Erin Thompson. I was visiting the mall today with my son. It was about 3 in the afternoon. There was supposed to be a big children's show called "Blast Off!" My son really wanted to see it. The ad said it would be a "science-fiction thriller." But a banner said the show was delayed. Workers hadn't finished the stage. My son and I were walking away when we passed a spaceman dressed all in white. His helmet had shiny, black glass in the front. He waved his arms at me and I guess he scared me a little, but my son was thrilled! Then the man went to the center of the mall and started yelling at some workers. It didn't sound like he was speaking English.

Source 3: Mall Manager Harold Zhou

My name is Harold Zhou. I am the manager of the mall. Today, we had to cancel a show we had planned at the mall. One of the actors for the show did not hear that the show was cancelled. He came to the mall. He was having trouble getting the helmet of his costume off, and he panicked. I understand he scared a few shoppers, but the situation is now under control.

Write an answer to each question.

1. What were the workers building in the center of the mall?

   _____

2. What did the alien look like?

   _____

Eyewitness Reports (cont.)

Write an answer to each question about the source material on page 60.

3. Was Justina right when she said that every mother was scared? How do you know?

   _____

4. Who do you think the alien was?

   _____

Here is the article a reporter wrote about the "alien" at the mall, using the information from the sources page 60. Read the article. Underline any fact that does not match something that one of the eyewitnesses said.

E.T., Phone Home!

Visitor From Another Planet, or...?

    Visitors to Woodside Mall had an unexpected close encounter today. A show that was to take place at one end of the mall was cancelled. An actor, Lee Hill, did not hear about the cancellation and showed up promptly at 3 P.M., dressed in his alien costume. When he saw the banner announcing the show's delay, he tried to take off the helmet of his costume, but it was stuck. A panicked Hill waved his arms and stopped a shopper, trying to get help. This started a panic as terrified shoppers fled the mall. One of them, Justina Reginald, reported that shoppers were screaming and fleeing from the alien attack. "I forgot all about shoe shopping," Justina said after the alien had grabbed her. Mall Manager Harold Zhou is quoted as saying, "The situation is now back to normal." The show, "Blasting Off," will take place Saturday at 2 P.M.

Rewrite each sentence that you underlined with the correct information from the sources.

5. _____

   _____

6. _____

   _____

7. _____

   _____

8. _____

   _____

9. _____

Name _____   Date _____

Life in Australia

Sources help the editor make sure that everything in the writing is correct. Sometimes the editor must check three sources. The sources may have different information.

Hannah wrote a report on Australia for her social studies class. She found three sources. Read the sources and then answer the questions on page 63.

Source 1: Map

Source 2: Article About Australian life

Many Australians live near the coast in the east, southeast, and southwest. The major cities are Sydney, Melbourne, Brisbane, Adelaide, and Perth. These cities are like other cities around the world. People living there do enjoy ocean-related sports, such as surfing and swimming.

But life in the *bush*, or countryside, is very different. This life is basically ranch life. Ranchers raise cattle or sheep. Sheep farmers, also called *graziers*, bring in crews once a year to shear the sheep for their wool. In the *outback*, the central part of Australia, ranches are very far apart. Ranchers sometimes have airplanes to get from one part of their land to another or to go to the nearest town for food and clothing. Radios are used to call doctors and to get emergency medical help. Two-way radios are used like telephones. And some ranch children go to school by radio! They listen to a radio program called *The School of the Air*. Their lessons are taught over the radio. Homework is mailed to the teachers.

Source 3: Glossary of Terms From Australia's Ranch Country:

barbie: an outdoor grill
brumbies: wild horses
buckjumpers: bucking broncos
bush: the remote countryside of Australia
matilda: a blanket roll

outback: the open country in the center of Australia
squatters: ranch owners
station: a ranch
tucker: food

Life in Australia (cont.)

Answer the questions about the sources on page 62.

1. Which source will be most important to Hannah in finding the location of the outback?
   a. source 1
   b. source 2
   c. source 3

2. After seeing these sources, what do you think will be the main focus of Hannah's report?
   a. the government of Australia
   b. life on stations in Australia
   c. life in the cities of Australia

3. How do you think that Hannah will use source 3?
   a. to add colorful language to her report
   b. to help her understand her report
   c. to help the reader learn more about Australian provinces

4. Here is a sentence from Hannah's report:

Squatters try to catch and tame matildas.

What might be wrong with this sentence?
   a. Hannah has used the wrong word for "ranch owner."
   b. Hannah has used the wrong word for "wild horses."
   c. Hannah has used the wrong word for "food."

5. Here is a section from Hannah's report:

Cities in Australia are much like cities everywhere. But *stations*, or ranches, in the remote countryside of Australia, are very different. These stations are far apart. *Squatters*, or ranch owners, sometimes use planes just to go shop for their groceries! Life in the outback can be lonely. Children sometimes have to use the radio to go to school. They listen to their lessons. Then they mail their homework to their teachers.

Which two sources did Hannah use to write this part of her report?

   a. sources 1 and 2
   b. sources 2 and 3
   c. sources 1 and 3

63   0-7424-2755-2 *Proofreading & Editing*

The Right Tool

A **checklist** is a list of items to edit in a piece of writing. This tool helps the writer find mistakes. Some mistakes, like grammar and capitalization errors, must be checked in all types of writing. Other mistakes must be checked only in some types of writing.

Read each question. Choose the correct answer or answers.

1. Which items would you edit in everything you write?

    a. spelling

    b. punctuation

    c. capitalization

    d. word choice

    e. clarity

    f. indenting

    g. extra or missing words

    h. appropriate for audience and purpose

2. Some errors appear in only some types of writing. What two items would you add to your checklist when editing a letter?

    a. match information with sources

    b. commas after the greeting and closing

    c. capitalization

    d. comma between date and year

3. Which item would not appear on a checklist for poetry?

    a. indenting

    b. capitalize the first letter of each line

    c. appropriate for audience and purpose

    d. punctuation

4. Which items would you find on a checklist for a story? Choose all that apply.

    a. capitalization

    b. quotation marks

    c. match the story with the source information

    d. punctuation

    e. spelling and homophones

    f. comma after the greeting

5. Which items would be important to check in a report?

    a. the report matches the source information

    b. topic and supporting sentences

    c. commas after the greeting and closing

    d. clarity

The Right Tool (cont.)

6. Read the selection. Use the checklist to edit. Use proofreading marks to fix the mistakes. Then answer the questions that follow. More than one correct answer is possible.

Checklist

☐ spelling   ☐ punctuation   ☐ topic sentence, supporting details, conclusion

---

Robert Louis Stevenson was a terrific author. He wrote some great adventure stories! The best one is called *Tresure island* and has a pirate named Long john Silver. Although Stevenson's characters can be scary, this story keeps the reader eager for more. Stevenson also wrote a childrens poetry book that I read when I was young.

7. Which of these errors are found using the checklist above?

    a. childrens

    b. Long john Silver

    c. Tresure

    d. missing conclusion: Someday, I hope to write like he did.

8. What other errors should be checked and corrected in this report?

    a. steps in correct order

    b. comma after greeting

    c. spelling

    d. capitalization

9. Use the following checklist to edit this portion of a story.

Checklist

☐ capitalization   ☐ indenting   ☐ quotation marks

The storm tumbled the ship as if it were nothing at all. "Captain alonzo, help! I'm caught in the ropes and can't free myself the sailor bellowed. But these words of desperation were swallowed by the angry wind. was all lost? Just then, the winds died down, and the rain slowed. This was not good. The crew of the *corona de Lisbon* was in the eye of the hurricane!

I'm Sorry

A **checklist** helps when you edit a piece of writing. A checklist for a letter has special additions. A comma separates the date and the year. One comma follows the greeting. Another comma follows the closing.

1. Use this checklist to edit the following letter. Use proofreading marks to fix the mistakes.

Checklist

- [ ] spelling
- [ ] punctuation
- [ ] comma between date and year

- [ ] comma after greeting and closing
- [ ] grammar
- [ ] indenting

April 3 2003

Dear Martina,

I hope you opend this letter and din't throw it away when you saw my adress on the envelope. Im writing to try to save our friendship from the awful mistakes I made. Before we can even attempd to build our friendship again, I need to apologize. I never knew thoses clay pots were part of your family collection. I should have been more careful The worst part is that I lyed when you asked me if I knew anything about the broken pots. The look on your face told me something was terribly rong. I was so afriad to tell you what I did that I lied If theres anything that friends should be able to count on, its honesty from each other. I miss our speshul times together, Martina. If you are willing to be my friend again, please write back.

You're friend always

Emma

2. The writer must always edit a letter for—
   a. capitalization
   b. comma between date and year

   c. elements of a story
   d. commas after the greeting and closing

     66   0-7424-2755-2 *Proofreading & Editing*

Letter to the Editor

A checklist for a letter is special. The list has more items. Look through the letter for each item on the checklist.

1.   Use the checklist to edit the letter below. Use proofreading marks to fix the mistakes.

Checklist

☐ spelling   ☐ comma after greeting and closing
☐ punctuation   ☐ grammar
☐ comma between date and year   ☐ indenting

1 East First, Apartment 1

Woodstock Illinois 60063

January 10 2001

Dear Editor

    thank you for your report on my stolun property. However, there are a few corrections that

need to be made to your article. Your paper claimed that my name is Chasing Horsey. The

correct name is Charles horsley. Also, your article stated that my bicicle was stolen on friday. Im

not sure whether or not you have noticed all of the snow outside. I was not riding my bike! My

snowmobile, though, has been missing since last Tusday. Finally, you reported that I am offering a

reward of $40,000, I could buy several new snowmobiles if I had that much money! Pleas print a

corect version of this report in next weeks paper. I look forward to reading some actual facts in

your paper.

Sincerly,

Charles Horsely

2.   What is the style or mood of this letter?

a. sincere   c. sarcastic

b. sad   d. cautious

A Business Deal

A writer often writes to explain something. The editor makes sure the information is clear and correct. The details must be in order.

Read the following explanation. Then answer the questions on page 69.

Laur's Aunt june opened a craft shop right on the corner of First and main. Aunt June invite Laur to sell her handmade quilted wall hangings in the store. but Laur didin't no how much to charge. With Aunt Junes help, Laur camed up with a way to figure out the best price.

The experment they designed had three steps.

Step 1: Figure out how much it costs to make a singel wall hanging by adding up the cost of the material thread and padding. When they finishd, they found that each hanging cost Laur about $6.00. Step 2: Sells the quilts for four diffrent prices for four saturdays in a row. X Laur put this information into a table Step 3: Figure the profit for each Saterday. Laur subtracted the cost of the quilt from the price she charged on that saturday to find her profit on each quilt. Then she multiplied her profit by the numbur of quilts she selled. Laur was very excited when thay looked at the results. At first, she told Aunt June that $7.00 might be the best price because they sold twelfe on that day. Aunt June thought $13.00 might be the best price. She explained that laur would only have to sell seven hangings each week to make $21.00. laur decited that was better than haveing to make twelve wall hangings each week.

	Saturday 1	Saturday 2	Saturday 3	Saturday 4
price each	$7.00	$10.00	$13.00	$16.00
profit each	$1.00	$4.00	$7.00	$10.00
number sold	12	7	3	1
total profit	$12.00	$28.00	$21.00	$10.00

A Business Deal (cont.)

Answer the questions about the explanation on page 68

1. Which detail in the explanation does not match the source?
   a. When Laur sold the quilts for $7.00, she sold only seven.
   b. Laur would make $28.00 if she sold seven quilts at $13.00 each.
   c. Laur would only have to sell three quilts a week to make $21.00.
   d. Laur could make more money if she sold the quilts for $10.00 each.

2. Could step 3 come before step 2 in this report? Why or why not?

   _____

   _____

   _____

   _____

3. Which sentence inserted at the X in step 2 would make the report clearer?
   a. Sell only the quilts Aunt June wanted to sell in her shop.
   b. Each Saturday have a different number of quilts available for sale.
   c. Sell the cheapest quilts the first Saturday.
   d. Record the price and the number of quilts sold.

4. Using the checklist below, edit the explanation. Always check for correct spelling, capitalization, and punctuation.

Checklist		
☐ spelling	☐ punctuation	☐ details in the correct order
☐ capitalization	☐ quotation marks	☐ grammar
	☐ clear and correct details	☐ indenting

5. Which item on the checklist did not need to be checked in this report?
   a. clear and correct details   c. quotation marks
   b. punctuation   d. capitalization

6. Explain why not.

   _____

Name _____   Date _____

A Journey in History

Reports give information. In a book report, the elements of the story must be explained. The writing should be clear and make sense to the reader. Does the report include the title and the author? Are the characters, setting, and conflict defined?

Read this report. Look for the elements of a story. Then, answer the questions on page 71.

A Journey in History

Do you like stories that are set in a real place and time in history. If you like historical fiction, youll like *Number the stars* by Lois Lowry. It is an outstanding book about a yung girls courage.

This story takes place in copenhagen Denmark in 1943. This were during World War II. At that time, germany was at war with many countrys. The German army took over Denmark. Annemarie, a ten-year-old girl lives in Denmark. She has a best freind named Ellen who is jewish. Annemarie had a sister named Lise. The Nazis did not like Jewish people. They wanted to torment the Jewish people in Denmark and take them away. Jews were often starved, beeten, or killed. The Jews in Poland were also tormented.

At first, the Nazis just insult Ellen and her family but soon the life threat was very real. How could Annemaries family save there Jewish friends? How culd they help Ellen's family escaped to a free country where they would be safe,

This story shows some of the horrors of the war, it also shows the courage it taked to protect the Jewish people from the Nazi soldiers. Even though she was only ten years old, Annemarie had to help her friend Was she successful? Did she have enouff courage to help ellen's family escape from the Nazis? My favrite part of the book is called the afterward. It is a section in the back of the book that tells some of the facts used in the story. Enjoying a book and lerning about histery at the same time is fantastic!

A Journey in History (cont.)

Answer the questions about the book report on page 70.

1. What is historical fiction?

   _____

   _____

2. Write the title and author of the book from the report. _____

   _____

3. What is the main character's problem? _____

   _____

How could this sentence be rewritten to help the reader understand who the Nazis were?

4. The German army took over Denmark.
   a. Germany took over Denmark.
   b. The Nazis, German soldiers, took over Denmark.
   c. Denmark took over the German soldiers.
   d. The German soldiers were called the Nazis. Together, they took over Denmark.

5. There are two sentences in this report that do not belong. Cross out the two sentences.

What is one detail that supports this topic sentence?

6. This story takes place in Copenhagen, Denmark, in 1943.
   a. The Nazis did not like Jewish people.
   b. At that time, Germany was at war with many countries.
   c. Annemarie had a sister named Lise.
   d. The Jews in Poland were also tormented.

7. Use this checklist to edit the report.

Checklist		
☐ spelling	☐ punctuation	☐ grammar
☐ capitalization	☐ clear and correct details	☐ indenting

Name _____   Date _____

Do You See the Problem?

Writers give information in reports. Reports must be clear and correct. The facts in the report must match the facts in the source, the place where the writer found the information.

Read the following report and sources. Then answer the questions on page 75.

Do You See the Problem?

More than nine million children around the world are at risk to go blind. Meny of these children live in Asia. in fact, 205,000 Asian children are blind becuse of a disease that is caused by poor nutrition. These children did not have to lose theyre sight. there is a solution to this tragic problem.

At the root of the problum is a diet low in vitamin A. A diet without enough vitamin A can cause blindness. The same shortage is also responsible for harmeng the skin, bones, and tooth. The health of a childs bones is very importent. To save the vision of children around the world, people need to learn to grow and shair the right foods with them. Many foods have high levels of vitamin A. Foods such as carots, sweet potatoes, and squash are excelent sources. Butter, cheese, and tuna also provide vitamin A. To fight this problem, all childrens need to eat the proper foods. good nutrition with vitamin A can help children keep their eyesight. Knoledge and action are the first steps.

Source 1: Asian Health Department Report, December 3, 2003

Low intake of vitamin A can cause a disease in the eye. This disease is called xerophthalmia. This disease affects more than five million children. It has caused 250,000 Asian children to lose their sight. In Asia, this is the major cause of blindness in young children. This shortage is most often seen in children from one to six years of age. Many suffer from a lack of vitamin A. Many also have the disease with the risk of blindness. Eating foods with higher vitamin A levels can put a stop to this disease.

Do You See the Problem? (cont.)

Read the chart. Then answer the questions below about the report on page 72

Source 2: Food Source Table

Sources of Vitamin A	Sources of Vitamin D
carrots, sweet potatoes, squash	egg yolks
broccoli, spinach, kale	liver
fish, liver	tuna
butter, egg yolks, cheese	milk

1. When writing a report, check that the facts in the report match the facts in the source. There are two mistakes in the report regarding the facts. List the mistakes. Then, edit the mistakes in the report.

Mistake 1: _____

Mistake 2: _____

_____

2. What is the main idea of the report?
   a. At least one cause of blindness is preventable with proper nutrition.
   b. Too much vitamin A can cause blindness in children.
   c. Blindness is caused by a lack of vitamin D.
   d. Asian children between one and six years of age are going blind.

3. Put a line through the sentence in the report that does not support the main idea.

4. Reread the report. Use the checklist to edit it. Use the source material to check the facts. Use proofreading marks to fix the mistakes.

Checklist

- ☐ spelling
- ☐ capitalization
- ☐ punctuation
- ☐ topic sentences and supporting details
- ☐ clear and correct details
- ☐ indenting
- ☐ facts match sources

---

     73   0-7424-2755-2 *Proofreading & Editing*

The End of an Empire

Reports give information, so they must be clear and correct. The facts in the report must match the facts in the sources.

Read the following report and timeline. Look at the map on page 75. Then answer the questions.

The End of an Empire

By 1493, the Inca people had bilt a vast empire. Their lands were in northwest South America. Inca towns was built along the Pacific coast and in the andes mountains. The Inca empire sprawled over 350,000 square miles. More than nine million people lived on Inca lands To hold the kingdom together, the Incas builded roads and bridges. They created ways to move food and goods from town to town. Theses developments helped the Inca empire to grow. They also helped the Inca empire to fall.

A spanish explorer named Pizarro came in 1532 He had heard tales of the Inca empire and he beleived the Incas had huge stores of gold. His ships landed on the Pacific coast, now part of peru. Pizarro led his soldiers allong the roads the Incas had built. The soldiers marched inland were they fought a battle. They continued along the roads to the Inca capital, Cusco. Pizarro and his army killed and looted along their journey. Although they killed many Incas, outhers may have fled Cusco and hid in machu picchu.

Once the Inca empire was beaten, Pizarro gone back to the coast. He followed the same roads out of the mountains and started his own city. His new capital city was called City of the Kings. This city is now called Abancay and is the capitol of Peru.

1525 – Explorers find Inca empire	1532 – Pizarro captures Cusco	1572 – Spanish armies defeat the last Inca army

1493 – Height of Inca Empire	1530 – Pizarro builds his army in Spain	1535 – Pizarro builds City of the Kings (Lima)

The End of an Empire (cont.)

1. Reread the report and use the checklist below to edit it. Use the source material (the timeline and the map) to check the facts. Use proofreading marks to fix the mistakes.

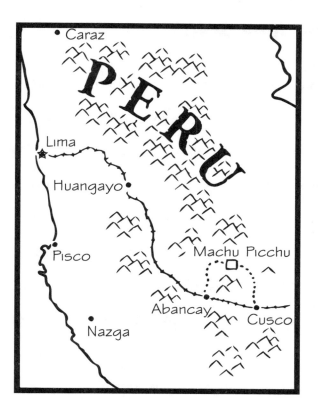

Checklist
- [ ] spelling
- [ ] capitalization
- [ ] punctuation
- [ ] grammar
- [ ] topic sentences and supporting details
- [ ] clear and correct details
- [ ] facts match sources

2. Check the facts in the report against the facts in the sources. Which fact in the report does not match?
    a. Pizzaro's ships arrived on the Pacific coast, now part of Peru.
    b. Some Incas fled the capital to hide in Machu Picchu.
    c. The soldiers continued along the roads to the Incan capital, Cusco.
    d. The City of the Kings is called Abancay.

3. What is the main idea of the second paragraph?
    a. A Spanish explorer named Pizarro came in 1532.
    b. Pizarro attacked the Incas to get their gold.
    c. The Incas built roads that the Spanish used.
    d. The Inca people hid from their attackers.

A Heritage Report

Reports give information, so they must be clear and correct. The facts in the report must match the facts in the sources.

Read the report. Look at the sources on this page and on page 77. Then answer the questions.

My Heritage by Tony Dossi

My whole family comes from "the old country," italy. My grandparents still life in the old country today. Although they travel to visit us, none of them would ever move awaye from the old country. My father and mother were both born in the old country. They both came to America in 1928 but they didn't know each other back then in 1928. My dossi grandparents live in a city called Florence. Grandmama dossi's name before she got marryed was Egine Valdo. They had my papa in 1964. He was olny eighteen when he left the old country. He came to America to go to school. Grandpapa Ciaco lives in the city of pisa, near the coast of Italy. There is a famous tower there that leans over. His wife was Wilma Mandoli and she came from the city of assisi, south of Florence. After my mama left the old country Grandmama Ciaco got sick. I never had the chance to meet her. I am proud that my family comes from Italy. They tell me wonerful stories about their lives there. It make me wish I lived there. one day, Id like to visit the places in Italy where my papa and mama grew up. Maybe I'll go back there to go to college when I'am older.

Source 1: Family Tree

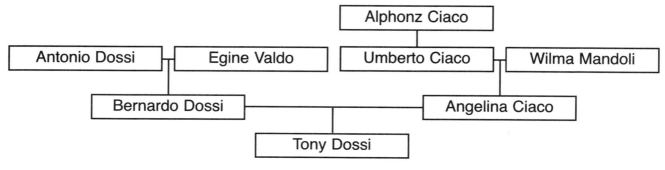

A Heritage Report (cont.)

Read the sources. Then answer the questions below about the report on page 76.

Source 2: Immigration Data for 1982

Name	Place of Birth	Date of Entry to U.S.
Bernardo Dossi	Florence, Italy	May 21, 1982
Angelina Ciaco	Pisa, Italy	October 16, 1982

Source 3:

Excerpt from a recorded interview with Grandpapa Ciaco

"I remember my papa telling me to go to America. He wanted our family to earn our fortune there. 'Umberto,' he would say to me, 'why do you want to stay here in the old country with so many poor people? Go to America where you can pick up the extra money from the ground.'

"I tried one time to go; I think it was in 1961. I was only twenty-one and I was ready for an adventure. Maybe it was 1962; I can't remember. What I do remember is that I met Wilma before I was ready to leave.

"Your mother, my Angelina, told me she was leaving for America. I knew my poor papa was getting his wish. It was sad for me, but I was happy for Angelina and for Papa, too."

1. There is a detail in Tony's report that is not correct. What is the detail?
   a. Tony's father was eighteen when he came to America.
   b. Tony's parents came to America in 1928.
   c. Umberto is Grandpapa Ciaco's first name.
   d. Grandmama Dossi's name before she got married was Egine Valdo.

2. What is the "old country?" _____

3. In the first paragraph, Tony uses the words "old country" too often. Think about other ways he could have kept the meaning without using those exact words. Edit the report to use "old country" only twice in the first paragraph.

4. Draw a line through the sentence in the report that does not tell about Tony's family.

5. Reread the report. Use the checklist to edit the report. Use proofreading marks to fix the mistakes.

Checklist

- [ ] spelling
- [ ] capitalization
- [ ] punctuation
- [ ] topic sentences and supporting details
- [ ] clear and correct details
- [ ] indenting
- [ ] facts match sources

On Top of Mount Rosa

Reports give information, so they must be clear and correct. The facts in the report must match the facts in the sources.

Read the report and the glossary for the experiment. Read the two other sources on page 79. Then answer the questions.

On Top of Mount Rosa

Purpose: This report tells how we performed our experiment on Mount rosa. The goal was to find out how cold it is on top of the mountain. We also measure how the air cooled along the way to the top. This report explain the equipment, the experiment, and the results.

Materials: Our team used three important pieces of equipment. First we used Josh's dads altimeter. The altimeter told us the altitude. Second, we used an outdoor thermometer from Lela's house. This told us how high above sea level we was. Third we had a compass, so we wouldn't get lost. we used Quentins science notebook to record results and notes.

Procedures: The experiment was easy to perform. we hiked up the trail and took measurements along the way. At first, we thought we needed to check the thermometer the whole time We soon learn that we only needed to check every 1000 feet.

Results: We found that the temperature at the base of Mount Rosa was 28.3 degrees C. At the top of the mountin the temperature was only 20 degrees at the top of the mountain. We also noticed something else. For every 100 feet of altitude, the air was about 1.6 degres coolerer. If we had known that befor, we wouldn't need an experiment. We would only have to know the height of mount rosa and the temprature at the base. This was a way cool thing to learn.

Source 1: Glossary of Terms

altimeter: a device used to measure altitude
altitude: the height above sea level, often measured in feet or meters
temperature: the amount of hotness or coldness of the air
thermometer: a device used to measure temperature

                   0-7424-2755-2 *Proofreading & Editing*

On Top of Mount Rosa (cont.)

Source 2: Mount Rosa Data

	Altitude	Temperature (°C)
base of Mount Rosa	4,280	28.3°
first measurement	5,000	27.2°
second measurement	5,280	26.7°
third measurement	6,280	25°
fourth measurement	7,280	23.3°
fifth measurement	8,280	21.7°
sixth measurement	9,246	20°

Source 3: Lab Notes

We keep taking the temperature, but it doesn't change. We're going to walk a long ways and try again. Maybe the thermometer is broken.	Well, another 1,000 feet and another 1.6 degree change. We think that the thermometer is working. So, the temperature must not change too much.
We went up 1,000 feet and the temperature changed. We will try again after another 1,000 feet. We still aren't sure it's working.	Lela tried taking the temperature in the shade. Then, she took it in the sun. It didn't seem to make any difference.

1. Reread the report. Use the checklist to help you edit the report. Use proofreading marks to fix the mistakes.

Checklist

☐ spelling   ☐ grammar
☐ capitalization   ☐ clear and correct details
☐ punctuation   ☐ facts match sources

2. Word choice is important in everything you write. What phrase in this report is not right for the audience?

    a. goal was to find out

    b. We also noticed something else.

    c. science notebook to record results and notes

    d. way cool thing to learn

Nothing but Trouble

A story is a special type of writing. It has a beginning, a middle, and an end. The setting, the characters, and a problem appear in the beginning of a story. Events happen in the middle of a story. The conflict is solved near the end of the story. Look for these parts in a story when you read.

Read the story. Then answer the questions on page 81.

The Rockford water disaster

Trouble, like a foxhound, alwyas seemed to track down the McKenzie twins. rusty and Roxie could count on problems with everything they did. Everyone in the town of rockford knew them as the "Truble Twins." But no one could have predicted the twins famus Rockford Water Disaster. On the day of Mr McKenzie's thirty-fifth birthday, Rusty and Roxie planned a suprise party. Rusty was in charge of decorations and muzic. He hung up balloons sparklers and bottle rockets. Roxie prepard all of the food and drinks. She had hot peppers, cheese and crackers, a huge cake, lemonade, and water. Thay rented a room in the Old town hotel. The room had a balcony that overlooked Center creek and a little bridge of stones. The party was a great succes with prezents, laughter, and lots of dancing. In fact it seemed to the guests that they were safe from the Trouble Twins' strange curse. everyone gathered as Roxie wheeled the massive cake into the center of the room. She lit the candles and everyone began to sing The real source of the trouble may have been Mr. carlisle. He bit into one of the hot peppers and howled! While he panted and waved his hands, Rusty reached for the pitcher of water. Unfortunately, Rusty bumped into the cake cart and the cart rolled into the wall. Unfortunatly, Rusty had set some of his decorations up against the wall, right where the cart now hit. Unfortunately, the candles on the cake lit the sparklers and bottel rockets. guests droped to the flooor. Bottle rockets whistled through the air, leaving smoky tails. Sparklers stuck into the cake, sending showers of sparks into the air.

Nothing but Trouble (cont.)

The room filled with smoke. Roxie pushed the cart through the slidding door and out onto the balcony. Unfortunately, the cart rolled all the way to the railing and jolted to a stop. Unfortunately, the cake and the platter saled over the railing and landed in Center creek Unfortunately, the cake and platter were to large to fit under the little Bridge. With the cake and platter stuck, the water from the creek began to clim out of its banks. When the sprinklers in the ceiling of the room turned on the guests ran down the stairs and out the door. however, as they bolted threw the door, they were greeted by a street full of water. The whole town was ankle-deep in Center Creek water! After some time, the cake finally crumbled. The waters of Center Creek sulked back into there banks. The town took four days to dry out. Everyone knew theyd never forget the Trouble twins famous party.

Reread the story to find the answers to these questions.

1. What is the conflict in the story?

   _____

   _____

2. How is the conflict resolved?

   _____

   _____

   _____

3. Word choice is important in everything you write. The word *unfortunately* appears six times in this story. Edit the story so it appears only once. Use your creativity to vary the sentences.

4. Edit the story using the checklist. Use proofreading marks to fix the mistakes.

Checklist

☐ spelling	☐ punctuation	☐ story elements
☐ capitalization	☐ beginning, middle, end	☐ indenting

Operation Sleep-In

When you edit a story, look for a beginning, a middle, and an end.
Check for quotation marks when a character speaks. Begin a new
paragraph when someone different speaks or a new idea begins.

Read the story. Then answer the questions on page 83.

Miss Loudmont marcht into our cabin at five o'clock in the morning and began to shout, Rise and shine, campers! Youve got a busy day ahead, and it all starts with mess at 0530. If you're going to shower, it's time to get moving now!" Her body pivoted sharply and then she marched off to anuther cabin.

Jessica was the first to start complaining. "next time someone wakes me up at five to tell me about a mess, I'm going…" "Mess is an old army term" explained monique. She waz always trying to show everyone how much she knew but nobody seem to care. "It means any mealtime, like breakfast, and it takes place in the mess hall."

I know," replied jessica, glaring at Monique. Jessica was the tough one. She was never afraid of anyone but always afraid of what the other girls thot. "I know a lot more than you probably do!" The peacekeeper in me couldn't stay out of the arguement, "Hey, settle down, you two. It's not worth fighting each other when it's old Army Sergeant Loudmouth that's causing the problem. She wakes us up too erly.

Jessica aimed her glare at me and asked, Just what do you think we can do about it, Miss Settledown" I was determined not to let Jessica see that I was afriad. Before I even knew what I was going to say, I answered, "Well, the real problem is that Miss Loudmont wakes up too early. so, all we need to do is make shure she sleeps in as late as possible." Then the whole plan sudenly unfolded in my mind.

Name _____ Date _____

Operation Sleep-In (cont.)

I kept my voice calm. "If we can keep her up too late and make sure her alarm doesn't go off, then we've got it made.

The three of us talked out all the details of the plan. That evening, we put Operation Sleep-In into action. after supper I asked Miss loudmont if we could sew tote bags for our books. Miss Loudmont was delited, and we were, too because that project kept us up late. while we were sewing, Jessica stole into Miss Loudmonts cabin and unpluged the clock. Just after midnight we said our goodnights to Miss Loudmont. "goodnight girls. See you bright and early" she said betweeen yawns. The next morning, a very flustered Miss Loudmont woke us up at 7:30 and dasht off to catch up with her day.

1. Use the checklist to edit this story. Remember to start a new paragraph when someone different speaks or when the main idea changes. Use proofreading marks to fix the mistakes.

Checklist

☐ spelling
☐ capitalization

☐ punctuation
☐ quotation marks
☐ beginning, middle, end

☐ story elements
☐ indenting

---

2. Imagine that Miss Loudmont caught Jessica unplugging her clock. Create your own ending to this story. Try to match the writer's style and language.

_____

_____

_____

_____

The Journal of Juan Ponce de León

Sometimes stories are written in journal form. In journal entries, one special task is to check that the dates have correct punctuation. This journal is a part of a story. The beginning, middle, or end may not be complete.

Read the story. Then answer the questions on page 85.

The Journal of Juan Ponce de León

July 3, 1521

Our narrow escape from these natives has gave the men quite a shock, and me as well. It certainly doesnt help matters that I was wounded by one of their arrows. Even though I feel downhearted, there is the promise of hope. Their attaks suggests that they are, in fact, guarding some treasure. Perhaps it is my long-sought-after Fountin of Youth. I've given orders to sail south. my task there shall be twofold. First and most importantly, I shall try to give my body the rest and attention it needs to heal. I expeckt to be able to return within three months' time. second, I will find a diffrent route and form a different plan We will find our way past these natives and locate the fountain they guard so closly.

July 20, 1521

I am now in Havana. Although I have sailed through unknown waters without fear, I are now afraid. my wounds do not heal. They are angry and read. My sleep is troubled my breathing harsh, and my pain extreme. The healers offer medicine and ointments, but my wounds seem beyond their skills What lies ahed for me, I cannot say. I find iit strange that the medicine I most need now comes from the fountain we have left behind.

The Journal of Juan Ponce de León (cont.)

July 23, 1521

How sad that people's the dreams are as frail as the people who dream them. with my death will my Fountain of Youth disapear into myth? My great desire is for the men to seek out that fountain and bring me it's life-giving waters. But I know they're is not time. my hope for healing flows from me along with my life. I had hoped that in Havana, I would find heeling. It has not been so. In seeking the treasure that gives life, mine has been taked.

1. Use the checklist to edit the journal. Use proofreading marks to fix the mistakes.

Checklist

☐ spelling   ☐ punctuation   ☐ elements of a story
☐ capitalization   ☐ dates for each entry   ☐ indenting
                 ☐ grammar

---

2. Name two ways a journal differs from a story.

_____

_____

_____

_____

3. What are the settings for these journal entries?

     a. at sea and in San Juan   c. in the mountains and on the beach

     b. at sea and in Havana   d. in China and in Japan

4. What is the main idea of the final entry?

     a. He is seeking treasure.   c. He is dying.

     b. He is thirsty and wants water.   d. He is seeking the Fountain of Youth.

5. On your own paper, write another entry for this journal. Date it six months earlier, when Ponce de León was planning his trip to look for the Fountain of Youth. Try to match the author's word choice and purpose for writing. When you are finished, use the checklist to edit your work.

Live Concert!

In a story, check for quotation marks and an indent whenever a new character speaks. Look for the story's beginning, middle, and end.

1. Read the story. Then, use the checklist to edit the story. Use proofreading marks to fix the mistakes.

Checklist

☐ spelling   ☐ punctuation   ☐ beginning, middle, ending
☐ capitalization   ☐ story elements   ☐ indenting
                    ☐ grammar   ☐ quotations

Oxygen for All: live Concert

"You can't not come in unless you have a backstage pass" grumbeld a tall man dressed in black. His eyes pulled us out of the crowd and sended us in the other direction. "How are we sposed to get any autographs? complained trevor. "I don't even know where to go buy one of those backstage passes anyway. Don't these people not know that Oxygen for All is my favorite group"

How could they know and why would they even care? askt Veronica. "Look, we've tryed every way we know how, but there's no way to get back there to see them."

veronica Trevor and I had already tried sneaking under the curtins on the sides of the stage. Trevor lifted the heavy, drapes while Veronica and I rolls underneath. His plan did not work out very well, however. A few security officers found us and made us leaf again. Next Trevor tried to bribe a security guard with twenty dollars. The guard was not amused. She shouted, "You cant pay me tweanty dollars and expect me to do something that would cost me my job. Get out of here, kid, befor you get thrown out for good"

finally, we tried to blend in with a large crowd moving through the security checkpoint. Thats

Live Concert! (cont.)

when the tall man told us we couldn't come in without a pass. Trevor was disappointed but he

trefused to gave up. he started talking to everybody: the Oxygen for All fans, theater employees,

even the guards. Everyone told him the same thing, "You need a pass, but I dont have one. As

Trevor was ready to give up, he saw three people walking out of the checkpoint. They wore huge

smiles and talk excitedly to each other. Trevor said, "did you actually get to go back stage to meet

them. Do you has any idea where I can get a backstage pass" The three fans immediately took

there backstage passes off and handed them to Trevor. "go for it, and take your friends! The

guys in Oxygen for All am so cool! you'll really like them.

Answer the questions about the story on page 86.

2. When does a new paragraph begin? Choose all that apply.
   a. when someone different speaks
   b. when the author chooses
   c. when there is a pause in the story
   d. when the main idea changes
   e. whenever there is a transition word

3. What happens in the beginning of this story? Remember to include the setting, the characters, and the conflict.

   _____

   _____

4. How do the main characters try to solve the conflict? Choose all that apply.
   a. They tried to steal passes from other people.
   b. They tried to blend in with a crowd.
   c. They tried to tempt a guard with money.
   d. They pretended they were sick.
   e. They tried to sneak under the curtains.
   f. They tried talking to everyone they could.

Name _____   Date _____

Achoo!

Poetry requires a special checklist. Editors must check all the items needed to edit a poem well.

Read the poem and answer the question that follows.

Pass the pepper, please!

They're once was a man in a whale

who wrote down his glorious tail...er...tale

Too send to his dad

But he was quite sad

when he found there wuz no way to mail.

Do you thenk this man sufferd despair

That he stompt and he hollered, "Not fare...er...fair?"

Hes no bellyacher,

with pepper in shaker,

He sent his dads leter Sneeze Air

1. Which checklist is best for editing this poem? _____

Checklist A	Checklist B
☐ spelling	☐ punctuation
☐ punctuation	☐ capitals in the title
☐ capitals in the title	☐ capitals to begin each line
☐ capitals to begin each line	☐ topic sentence and supporting details
☐ quotation marks	☐ date in the heading

2. Use the checklist you chose to help you edit the poem.

Name _____   Date _____

The Wheelchair

Poetry requires a special checklist. Editors must check all the items needed to edit a poem well.

Read this poem. Then, use the checklist below to edit it.

While staring down the slope to the beach

I find myself there, standed in the waves

The cold water shocks my skin and toss's me

Tumbeling, rolling in blue-green excitement.

I turn my gaze to the forests and spy me their,

A child of the green, ranning through cool shade

Squirrels play game with me, from branch to branch,

Trunk to trunk, we leap and cling, climbing and dash.

My eyes finds a looking glass but I can't not find myself

In the reflection. I sea only a small child

Sitting on a chrome seat with large, gray wheeels

I dreams my dreems for him

and he smiles as if he knows.

Checklist

☐ spelling   ☐ capitals to begin each line   ☐ grammar
☐ capitalization   ☐ punctuation

89   0-7424-2755-2 *Proofreading & Editing*

Name _____ Date _____

Time Machines in the Attic

Poetry requires a special checklist. Editors must check all the items needed to edit a poem well.

1. Read the poem. Use the checklist to edit it. Then answer the questions on page 91.

Checklist

- [ ] spelling
- [ ] capitals in title
- [ ] capitals to begin each line
- [ ] punctuation
- [ ] extra or missing words
- [ ] grammar

(1) In photo albums high on shelves,

in in attics, closets, tucked away,

We look for memories of ourselfs

to travel back too yesterday.

(2) A <u>snapshot</u> in a dusty frame

Reveals a few tuxedoed men;

Whil father trys to find each name,

He tells you how it was back then.

(3) For somewere in the mind still lurks

the joy and sorrow long since past.

The freinds and foes, the a jocks and jerks,

Combine to make the memorys last.

(4) So when you find that silly hats

Or read the <u>ancient</u> magazines,

Rememember in each trinket that

you hold the keys to time machiines.

90 0-7424-2755-2 *Proofreading & Editing*

Name _____ Date _____

Time Machines in the Attic (cont.)

Answer the questions below about the poem on page 90.

2. Look at the items on the checklist. Which of these should be included on checklists for all types of writing? (Hint: Include stories, reports, poems, and letters.)
   a. capitals to begin each line, correct spelling, punctuation
   b. quotation marks, capitals in title, correct spelling, sentence end marks
   c. punctuation, correct spelling, quotation marks, extra or missing words
   d. capitals in title, capitals to begin each line, correct spelling, extra or missing words

3. Which item on this checklist is only found on a checklist for poetry?
   a. punctuation
   b. capitals in the title
   c. extra or missing words
   d. capitals to begin each line

Word choices are very important in poetry. Two words are underlined in the poem's numbered stanzas. Choose a different word that means nearly the same as the underlined word. To choose the best word, find one that matches the style of the poem as well as the meter or rhythm.

4. In the second stanza, "snapshot" could be replaced with _____
   a. picture
   b. photograph
   c. painting
   d. slingshot

5. In the fourth stanza, "ancient" could be replaced with _____
   a. old
   b. powerful
   c. antique
   d. yellowed

6. In stanza 3, the phrase "jocks and jerks" does not seem to fit. These are slang terms. What words might fit the theme of this poem better?
   a. the good and bad
   b. the smiles and smirks
   c. the kind store clerks
   d. the athletes and unpleasant folks

7. What are the "time machines" found in attics?
   a. machines that can take a person back in time
   b. photographs and magazines only
   c. machines, like heaters or air conditioners, often found in attics
   d. anything that brings back memories

0-7424-2755-2 Proofreading & Editing

Back to Basics

Different types of punctuation are the road signs of writing. They tell the reader if someone is speaking. They tell the reader to slow down. They also tell the reader when a thought is complete. Capital letters also help readers identify different kinds of information. Correct spelling helps keep writing clear and easy to read.

Choose the correct word or words to complete these sentences.

1. (All though, Although) Corinne is her best friend, Allie asked Carl to the Electric Jellyfish concert.

2. Carl really loves to listen to (there, their, they're) music.

3. The Jellyfish concert was (grate, great); especially the last (peace, piece) they played.

4. Both Allie and Carl would love to hear the band play (agin, again).

Choose the correct answer. Which sentence contains no spelling errors?

5. a. The biplane's engine rumbled as we wated at the end of the runway.
   b. Finally, we recieved the OK to take off.
   c. The engine sputtered and, just as suddenly, purred as we took off.
   d. We peered betwine the wings down to the miniature town below.

Use proofreading marks to edit these sentences for the correct use of capitals.

6. on july 20, 1969, an american was the first person to step on the moon.

7. we used to live in dallas, texas, at 772 congress drive.

8. "there is no heat," rico noted at midday. "it is still 15 degrees below zero."

Circle the choice that shows correct capitalization.

9. a. My favorite book is titled *a wrinkle in time*.
   b. a very talented author named Madeleine L'Engle wrote it.
   c. Don remarked, "that book is a wonderful fantasy."
   d. My aunt gave me my own copy of the book on my birthday, August 12.

Back to Basics (cont.)

Circle the choice that shows the correct punctuation.

10. a. December 7, 1941, is a date that will live in infamy.
    b. "Would you please get me a towel? asked Fabian as he stepped out of the pool.
    c. With a shovel and a tree Ranger Mark began the Forest Service project.
    d. My family and I will travel to Barrow Alaska next summer.

11. a. It was delivered to 55 Temple Rd on December 19, 2000.
    b. Mrs Sweger will have chocolate and I will have strawberry, please.
    c. "Hey," the hurt city worker cried, "can anybody hear me."
    d. Happier than ever, Danica married her true love, Jeff.

Rewrite these sentences using the correct spelling, punctuation, and capitalization.

12. after hearing the instrucshuns we stil didnt know how to drive to dr kirks howse

_____

_____

13. mr ingham studyed at hiram law school iin standsbury connecticut

_____

_____

14. In what types of writing should you edit for spelling, punctuation, and capitalization?
    Choose all that apply.

    a. stories   d. instructions   g. explanations

    b. letters   e. lists   h. notes

    c. reports   f. homework   i. poems

15. In what types of writing would you edit for commas after the greeting and closing?

    a. stories   c. reports

    b. letters   d. instructions

16. Quotation marks are most likely to be found in what type of writing?

    a. letters   c. stories

    b. instructions   d. explanations

Name _____   Date _____

Yours, Mine, Theirs, or Ours?

To show possession:

Add an **apostrophe** and an **s** to:

    most singular nouns: cat**'s** tail, Jim**'s** snake

    singular nouns ending in **s**: bus**'s**

    plural nouns that do not end in **s**: children**'s** toys

Add only an apostrophe to:

    plural nouns ending in **s**: pant**s'** pocket

Rewrite each group of words to show ownership. The first one is done for you.

1.   the toys belonging to Mary   Mary's toys

2.   a house belonging to Becky _____

3.   the place in history belonging to the cold war _____

4.   the score of the players _____

5.   the shoes belonging to the baby _____

6.   a game belonging to the children _____

7.   the cat belonging to Aleah _____

8.   the car belonging to Mrs. Marx _____

9.   the bus belonging to the city _____

Use proofreading marks to edit the underlined words for correct possessive use.

10.   The <u>students</u> test scores were the finest in the county.

11.   The group of students hurried over to study at <u>Shireen</u> house.

12.   Those <u>cats</u> collars were ruined in the downpour.

            0-7424-2755-2 *Proofreading & Editing*

Remember the Alamo!

In all writing, the subject and verb must agree. Some verbs follow a pattern. Others do not follow a pattern and must be memorized.

Read these sentences. Choose the sentence in which the subject and verb agree.

1. a. Pablo and I winned a trip to the Alamo in Texas!

    b. Our sponsors telled us that we were each allowed to bring one person with us.

    c. Since our fathers both teach history, we invited them.

2. a. The 747 lifted off early in the morning.

    b. We was so excited that the early hour simply didn't matter.

    c. Soon, we touches down in San Antonio.

3. a. A cab were there waiting to whisk us away to our hotel on the Riverwalk.

    b. After checking in, we hurried along the banks of the river toward the Alamo.

    c. Pablo and I leaded the way up the stairs from the Riverwalk.

4. a. Pablo's father seen the wall of the Alamo before anyone else.

    b. Suddenly, we all broked into a run.

    c. I could hardly believe that the Alamo was right there in front of us!

Read each sentence. Circle the correct form and tense of the verb.

5. As soon as we (enters, entered) the building, everything became quiet.

6. The Alamo (demand, demanded) respect.

7. How exciting to (see, sees) where so many brave people (gived, gave) their lives for freedom!

8. Even volunteers from other states (comed, came) to the Alamo to fight.

Use proofreading marks to fix the following sentences.

9. Wouldn't it be wonderful if the walls of the Alamo could told their secrets?

10. Dad ask me if I think that I would have been brave enough to fights.

11. I'm not sure, but I imagines I would be as courageous as the heroes of the Alamo.

12. I will always remembered our incredible trip!

A High-Tech Gift of Memories

In writing, all sentences must be complete. They must be grammatically correct. They must also have the words in the correct order to make sense.

Circle the letter of the sentence that is grammatically correct.

1.
a. Matti and Kim are creating a DVD with the newest technology.

b. Creating a DVD Matti and Kim are with the newest technology.

c. With the newest technology, creating a DVD Matti and Kim are.

d. Matti and Kim creating a DVD with the newest technology are.

2.
a. First, old pictures that people sent them they are scanning images.

b. They are scanning from old pictures that people sent them first images.

c. First, they are scanning images from old pictures that people sent them.

d. From old pictures that people sent them, they scanning images are.

Use proofreading marks to fix the grammatical mistakes in these sentences.

3. After the pictures are scanned onto the computer

4. The next step in the process is to the pictures in the order they choose.

5. The technology makes very easy this step.

6. Once the images in order are, transitions are added.

7. In a pleasing way the transitions from one picture to another move.

8. Sound creation is next, they record music, that they play.

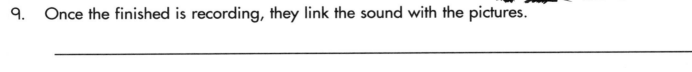

Rewrite these sentences so that they are grammatically correct.

9. Once the finished is recording, they link the sound with the pictures.

_____

_____

10. Movie technology with Matti and Kim create a very special gift for their parents.

_____

_____

A Trip to Diver's Cove

Editing sentences requires knowing what to look for in each type of sentence.

Fragments must be rewritten as complete sentences.

Simple sentences must have capitals and end marks.

Compound sentences require a comma to divide the two independent clauses.

Complex sentences often have clauses set off by commas.

Run-on sentences must be cut into two sentences or connected with a comma and a conjunction.

Write the type of sentence on the line. Then use proofreading marks to edit the sentences.

_____1. Putting on her snorkel and mask Jennifer explored the cove.

_____2. She spied a sea anemone moving gently with

_____3. Her brother joined her, they snorkeled toward the rocks.

_____4. Suddenly, Jennifer saw something moving.

_____5. Motioning to her brother Jennifer looked more closely.

_____6. One tentacle rose and another appeared.

_____7. a miniature octopus peeked at the children.

_____8. Just as suddenly as it appeared it disappeared!

_____9. After they explored the rocks

Circle the letter of the sentence with no errors.

10.   a. As if the octopus wanted them to play he followed along the ocean's floor.

      b. Jennifer noticed that it was the same octopus, it had a brown spot that looked like a pickle over the top of its head.

      c. Jennifer and her brother swam back to play with

      d. Are all octopi as friendly as the one in Diver's Cove?

Name _____   Date _____

The Spice of Life!

Using the same type of sentence over and over bores the reader. Edit all writing to vary the sentences. Vary the length of the sentence, as well as the type. As always, use correct spelling, capitalization, and punctuation.

1. Create complex or compound sentences by combining these short sentences into one or two new sentences.

   The meteor hurdled toward the earth. It tore the black night. It fell to the ground. It created a hole where it landed.

   _____

   _____

2. A sentence must be a complete thought. Finish the following thought to make a complete sentence.

   When Ashti and Hannah witnessed the meteor fall, _____

   _____

3. Sometimes a writer combines too many thoughts. Rewrite this sentence correctly by breaking it into sentences that make sense.

   The meteor landed and Ashti and Hannah cautiously explored the area so they could examine it but they couldn't find it.

   _____

   _____

   _____

4. Using a dependent clause at the start of a sentence is a good way to vary the type of sentence. Rearrange this sentence by putting a dependent clause at the beginning.

   The meteor split the darkness of night as it broke into the earth's atmosphere.

   _____

   _____

   _____

One Idea at a Time

A **paragraph** is a group of sentences that tells the reader about one main idea. It has a topic sentence, supporting sentences, and a concluding sentence.

Choose the best concluding sentence for the paragraph.

1.   Sometimes the difference between success and failure is *one*. One point, one grade, one second, one inch, or one person can make all the difference. The people who always seem to succeed understand this. The Principle of One means that if you can do just one more, you could make the difference. Since you get to decide whether you will do one more, you get to decide whether you will win more often.

   a. *One* is a concept that can improve your life.

   b. Sometimes, the difference between success and failure is *one*.

   c. Examples can be found everywhere there are successful people.

When beginning a new paragraph and main idea, signal the reader by using transitions. **Transitions** draw attention to the new idea.

Read the following paragraphs. Choose the best sentence to transition from one paragraph to the next.

2.   Many examples of the Principle of One come from the world of sports. Think about Wilt Chamberlain who scored 100 points in a single basketball game. What if he scored one less? Sports gives us story after story of the Principle of One.

   a. However, athletics is not the only place we can see this principle in action.

   b. Finally, another area of life gives examples of how this principle is used.

   c. One more "thank you" or one more "have a nice day" can be even more important.

3.   This principle is alive in day-to-day life as well. Opening the door for one more person or saving one smile for someone with a frown could be the one gift that person needed. When people give one more, they will receive one more. The Principle of One is the secret to a happy life.

   a. Choose to avoid the Principle of One and watch your life change for the better.

   b. With so many people failing, it is hard to believe the Principle of One.

   c. In the end, the choice to live by the Principle of One is a choice each person makes.

◆◆◆◆◆◆◆◆◆◆◆◆◆◆◆◆◆◆◆◆◆◆◆◆◆◆◆◆◆◆◆◆◆◆◆◆◆◆

What's the Point?

Every piece of writing is different. A letter to a friend uses different words than a letter to a teacher. The words a writer chooses must match the **purpose** and the **audience**.

◆◆◆◆◆◆◆◆◆◆◆◆◆◆◆◆◆◆◆◆◆◆◆◆◆◆◆◆◆◆◆◆◆◆◆◆◆◆

Read the purpose and choose the best topic sentence.

1. explaining grammar to your parents
   a. In Oxford, they teach a different comma use than in Cambridge.
   b. You have to put a comma before the *and* in a compound sentence.
   c. Grammar has changed with the language and helps us to exchange ideas clearly.

2. story about a jungle village in South America
   a. The shaman danced around the fire, singing.
   b. Some tribes in South America rely on their shamans for health care.
   c. Shamans wear masks, and they search through the jungle for roots.

3. Choose the type of closing used in a letter to a store manager.
   a. Yours forever,   b. With love,   c. Sincerely,

4. Choose the type of closing used in a letter to your favorite cousin.
   a. Yours,   b. Best regards,   c. Sincerely,

5. Which choice uses appropriate words for a report about space?
   a. We have so much to learn from space that I get very excited.
   b. Space exploration is the next great adventure for humankind.
   c. Wouldn't it be awesome to find bug-eyed creatures somewhere out in space?

Rewrite this sentence for each type of writing. Remember to use appropriate words.

We sailed around the world.

6. a letter to your jealous friend _____

_____

7. a newspaper article _____

_____

0-7424-2755-2 *Proofreading & Editing*

Tell Me Why

A **paragraph** is a group of sentences that tells the reader about one main idea. It has a topic sentence, supporting sentences, and a concluding sentence. An editor must check that all the sentences support the main idea. This is especially important when the paragraph expresses an opinion.

Read each opinion. Choose which reason supports that opinion best.

1. People should never litter.
  a. Air pollution is one possible cause of lung cancer.
  b. Many forms of garbage can harm the soil or wildlife.
  c. I don't like the way it looks when trash is everywhere.

2. Musicals are more enjoyable than movies.
  a. The floors in movie theaters are always covered with old candy and popcorn.
  b. Movies have great special effects that can bring the viewer into the story.
  c. After a musical, the audience gets to take the memory of the songs home with them.

3. Water skiing is harder than snow skiing.
  a. Before the boat pulls you, the waves can knock your skis out of position.
  b. The threat of collision with trees and other skiers is frightening.
  c. Both types of skiing offer challenges and thrills.

Write three reasons that support the following opinion. Circle the letter of the reason you feel best supports the opinion.

4. A safari vacation would be more fun than a beach vacation.

  a. _____

  b. _____

  c. _____

5. Choose one of these opinions. Support it with three reasons.

Opinion A: On the weekend, I like to relax with a good book or talk with a good friend.

Opinion B: On the weekend, I like to get out and do something adventurous.

_____

_____

_____

    0-7424-2755-2 *Proofreading & Editing*

◆◆◆◆◆◆◆◆◆◆◆◆◆◆◆◆◆◆◆◆◆◆◆◆◆◆◆◆◆◆◆◆

Splasher

When you edit, you can make your own checklist for each type of writing.

◆◆◆◆◆◆◆◆◆◆◆◆◆◆◆◆◆◆◆◆◆◆◆◆◆◆◆◆◆◆◆◆

Make your own checklist to edit the letter. Be sure to include the punctuation that follows the greeting and closing. Edit the letter using your checklist and the proofreading marks you have learned.

June 29 2002

Dear miss Joslyn

    Oh, thank you thank you, a bazillion times thank you! Uncle Richard and aunt Carol just told me that you've agreed to sell us the Arabian colt. I wanted to write immediately to let you know how excited I am. This is easly the best day of my entire life I promise you I'll do evrything you taught me at your riding school. Ive alredy started building the fence to separate part of the medow. I'll make sure the brook cuts threw the colts area since he likes splashing so much. In fact maybe his name should be about splashing. I'll has to think a little more about that when I'm not so excited. Uncle Richard says he'll set up the trailer and well start driving by saturday. Since it normally takes about three days, we'll probly see you on Tuesday. Please taked care of my new horse, splasher, until I get there.

thanks you again

Shawna

Checklist

☐ _____   ☐ _____   ☐ _____
☐ _____   ☐ _____   ☐ _____
                            ☐ _____

◆◆

A Letter Home

When you make a checklist for editing a letter, be sure to look for mistakes that happen only in letters.

◆◆

Make your own checklist to edit the letter. Edit the letter using your checklist and the proofreading marks you have learned.

Cambrai, France

November 25 1917

My dearest Mother and Father,

    I'm off duty for a fortnight, so I finly have a little time to write. please write to tell me that everything is wonderful in La Rochelle. Every day Im here I think about when I will retrun to you and the simple life at home. I long for all the things I used to dread, even scraping the barnacles from the ship. Tell jacques I look forward to helping hiim with the nets after my return. I was doubtful about when I might be able to return, but this last week have lifted my spirits. The british stormed the battlefield with mor tanks than I have ever seen. Thay trampled across open meadows and drove the germans back. my troop fell in behind the tanks and followd them for several miles. If the British ceep pushing hard, maybe we can finish this war before the summer. I will write again soon. For now I'll cherish the thought of you reeding this letter in comfort. If I had to, I wood give my life to keep the German army far away from my family.

love always

Pierre

Checklist

☐ _____   ☐ _____   ☐ _____
☐ _____   ☐ _____   ☐ _____

          0-7424-2755-2 *Proofreading & Editing*

The Road to Wonderland

When you make a checklist to edit a report, remember the report must be clear and correct. The editor must check the facts in a report. The facts must match the facts from the sources.

Read the report and the sources here and on page 105. Then, answer the questions on page 105.

The road to Wonderland

Ask a child how to get to Wunderland and he may tells you, "You go threw the looking glass." From Alices point of view, he would be exactly right. However, the first road to Wonderland wasn't not as easy as stepping through a looking glass. That first road was paved, word by word, by a man named Charles Dodgson, also knowed as Lewis Carroll.

The real road to Wonderland starts in Cheshire england. That is were Charles Dodson was born in 1832. He went to school at Rugby and then to the University of Oxford His field of study was math but his love was entertaining children. Perhaps this is why he chose a diffrent name for his writing career. Charles Dodgson was the math techer and Lewis Carroll was the author.

Charles Dodgson loved to write letters. He mailed thousends during his life. In his letters to children, he sended drawings and fantastic ideas. It was this love four childrens and fantasy that began his writing career In 1871 he published the book "Alice's adventure in wonderland." When he did this, he announced to children that the road to Wonderland was open. Ever since, children have walks his road. that is why the real road to Wonderland gose through the minds of readers around the world.

Source 1: List of Charles Dodgson's Publications

1865: *Alice's Adventure in Wonderland* by Lewis Carroll
1869: *Phantasmagoria and Other Poems* by Lewis Carroll
1871: *Through the Looking Glass and What Alice Found There* by Lewis Carroll
1876: *The Hunting of the Snark* by Lewis Carroll
1879: *Euclid and His Modern Rivals* by Charles Dodgson
1893: *Sylvie and Bruno* by Lewis Carroll

The Road to Wonderland (cont.)

Source 2: Timeline

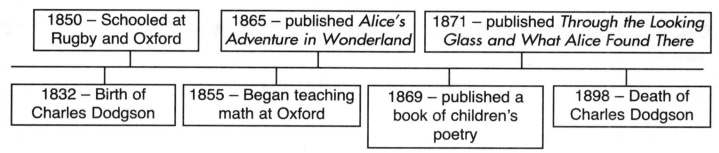

| 1850 – Schooled at Rugby and Oxford | 1865 – published *Alice's Adventure in Wonderland* | 1871 – published *Through the Looking Glass and What Alice Found There* |

| 1832 – Birth of Charles Dodgson | 1855 – Began teaching math at Oxford | 1869 – published a book of children's poetry | 1898 – Death of Charles Dodgson |

1. A biography is a type of report. Create a checklist to remind you of the items you need to check in a report. Then, use your checklist to edit the report on Charles Dodgson.

Checklist

☐ _____   ☐ _____   ☐ _____
☐ _____   ☐ _____   ☐ _____
☐ _____   ☐ _____

Answer the questions about the report.

2. Which fact in the report does not match the timeline?
   a. Charles Dodgson was a math teacher.
   b. Charles Dodgson was born in 1832.
   c. In 1871, he published the book *Alice's Adventure in Wonderland*.
   d. He went to school at Rugby and then the University of Oxford.

3. What is the main idea of the third paragraph?
   a. how Charles Dodgson wrote many letters
   b. how Charles Dodgson became a writer for children
   c. that Charles Dodgson could draw fantasy pictures
   d. that Charles Dodgson wrote fantasy letters to children in his spare time

4. What was the title of the author's book on math?

   a. *Phantasmagoria and Other Poems*   c. *Euclid and His Modern Rivals*

   b. *The Hunting of the Snark*   d. *Sylvie and Bruno*

One Problem or Another

When you make a checklist to edit a report, remember the report must be clear and correct. The editor must check the facts in a report. The facts must match the facts from the sources.

Read this report and the sources on page 107. Then, follow the instructions on page 107.

Solving One Problem

Often, when one problem is solved, a new problem is created. The automobile helped people to be more mobile but is now one of the gratest sources of air pollution. Pesticides can kill bugs, but they also hurt human beans. You can see the way one problem can create anuther in regard to fast foods. In the last twenty years, our lives have become very busy. Often while people drive from place to place, they do not have enough time to stop to eat a good lunch. Restaurants like Bills Burgerama have solved this problem. "The fast food business has helped americans to eat quickly during there busiest days.

But problems have come out of this solution. Because of our eating habits, Americans are having health problems. Marquita Jells, a nutrition expert, says, "Heart diseese is the number won killer in our country today. The number of Americans with wieght problems is on the rise. Someone eats a burger from Bills Burgurama and then sits in the car and eats it. That person doesn't not have the chance to exercise." Whats the answer? Maybe we need fast food thats also good food. Jells says, "Imagine a drive-throo with tofu hot dogs and crunchy carrot sticks!" Maybe Jells is right when she says it would be better to go hungrey instead. But we need to find a solution that doesnt make another problem instead.

One Problem or Another (cont.)

Read these sources for the article on page 106. Then answer the questions.

Source 1: Interview with Marquita Jells, nutritionist

"Fast food is a disease that has spread across America. This is how I see the problem. Heart disease is the number-one killer in our country today. The number of Americans with weight problems is on the rise. Someone eats a burger from Bill's Burgerama and then sits in the car and eats it. That person doesn't have the chance to exercise. And we know that exercise helps us stay healthy. We need to look at the fast food problem in a positive way. Let's have restaurants that give us healthy food. Imagine a drive-through with tofu hot dogs and crunchy carrot sticks! Then people who grab a quick lunch wouldn't end up with health problems."

Source 2: Interview with Bill Maxon, president of Bill's Burgerama

"Americans are busy people. They run from job to job, from daycare to school, and to countless stores. While they are busy living their lives, we are here to take care of their hunger. The fast-food business has helped Americans to eat quickly during their busiest days. Without fast foods, people might get less done, or, even worse, they might have to go hungry!"

1. What in the report must be changed to match the information in the sources?

   a. quotes   b. numbers   c. facts

2. Explain the error in the report on the lines below. Then edit the report to make sure it matches the sources.

   _____

   _____

3. The last sentence of the report is weak. Rewrite it so that it makes a stronger conclusion to the article and ties in with the thought of solving a problem.

   _____

   _____

4. Create your own checklist to edit this report. Then, use the checklist to edit for all errors. Is the information correct? Do topic sentences have supporting details?

Checklist

☐ _____	☐ _____	☐ _____
☐ _____	☐ _____	☐ _____
	☐ _____	☐ _____

◆◆◆◆◆◆◆◆◆◆◆◆◆◆◆◆◆◆◆◆◆◆◆◆◆◆◆◆◆◆

Peace, At All Costs

To edit a story, your checklist should include the elements of a story. Do the characters speak? Is the story complete? Do paragraph breaks make sense?

◆◆◆◆◆◆◆◆◆◆◆◆◆◆◆◆◆◆◆◆◆◆◆◆◆◆◆◆◆◆

Read the story. Then follow the instructions on page 109.

Peace, At All Costs

King Reginald of Dunland and his guide, Sir nelson Wren, looked across the foggy field. They could hear the shouts and clatter of the army on the other side of the meadow. The thick air choke their visibility to less than twenty yards.

"It should never have come to war" King reginald muttered to himself. "There are far too many good people and good reasons for us not to battle today.

Sir Nelson paused, trying to decide whether or not he should speak. Finly, he said, "Sire, what else could you possibly have don to prevent this encounter? Was it not you who made the long journy to his castle to try to settle the dispute? Did you not offer to help him build the roads and the bridges that would increse trade to his kingdom? You even offered your own son to serve and advise King Arnold. what more could you have done, Sire?" A young boy courageously began to beat a drum. He was barely visible in the fog. "Whatever I tried before, said King Reginald, "was clearly not enough." He kicked his heels into the sides of his stallion and bolted into the fog. "arnold!" cried the king's lone voyce in the fog, Arnold, I am coming to you without soldiers or arms. We are not going to fight today. Arnold, where are you?"

King Arnold accepted the pleas of King Reginald and met him on the battlefield. "What ho, reginald? qestioned Arnold cautiously. He moved forward. "Arnold, we cannot risk the lives of our brave soldiers. We have not looked hard enogh for another answer. To save these soldiers and their families from war, I will make this offer. I will directs every trade caravan from my kingdom through your lands. I will tell them to bye your goods and offer fair prices so your people will

Peace, At All Costs (cont.)

prosper. let us provide these soldiers incomes and hopes rather than swords and shields. What

say you, Arnold? Arnold pawsed. The world seemed to hold its breath, waiting for his answer.

"I tell you, Reginald, it shall be as you say. we shall make peace on this foggy feild, not war."

Answer these questions about the story.

1. What is the setting of the story? _____

2. What is the conflict in the story? _____

   _____

   _____

3. The climax of a story leads to the resolution of the conflict. It is the highest point of
    excitement. It occurs right before the end. What sentence tells the climax of the story?
    a. "We shall make peace on this foggy field, not war."
    b. The entire world seemed to hold its breath, waiting for his answer.
    c. "I tell you, Reginald, it shall be just as you say."
    d. "What more could you have done, Sire?"

4. What is the resolution to the conflict in the story?

   _____

5. Dialogue, the speech of different characters, often needs editing in stories. A new
    paragraph should start each time a new character speaks. How many paragraphs should
    this story have?

    a. four   c. seven

    b. five   d. nine

6. Create a checklist to edit this story. Then use it to edit for all errors. Do the characters
    speak? Are the paragraph breaks correct?

Checklist

☐ _____   ☐ _____   ☐ _____
☐ _____   ☐ _____   ☐ _____
              ☐ _____

A Story Within a Story

Chapters of a story include a beginning, middle, and an end, just like a complete story.

Read the following chapter of a story. Think about what must be put on a checklist for a story. Remember to look for the elements of a story. Then follow the instructions on page 111.

Chapter 7: In Search of Khanni

The thin trail slithered through the heavy undergrowth. A canopy of giant leafes kept the sunlight out and held in the heavy heat. Indiko Umboti paused to listens to the sounds of the jungle. He knew he could not depend on his eyesight here on the dark winding trail. He lisened carefully for too much silence or too much noise Nothing out of the ordinary camed to his ears, so he continued quickly down the path.

suddenly the ground opened up and swallowed him. Time froze as Indiko tumbled awkwardly into the open air. He watched in slow motion as the floor of the pit rushed up to crush into his body. Indiko lay confused. scarlet pain shouted from hiis ankle and arm. Soon, his mind climbed into the pit with him and he understould what had happend. He had fallen into an animal pit dug by one of the local tribes.

Indiko soon began to understand that his problem were more serious than a mere tumble into a hole. The pit was about twelve feet deep with hard, steep walls of soil. normally, a few footholds and a jump might get him out, but the other problum was his ankle Indiko probed the pain-filled joint with his long, slender fingers Even if he could get out, he would be easy prey for any animal that chose to hunt him. He decited to lay and wait for the tribe to find him.

The afternoon drifted by slowly and melted into evening. A blacker darkness seeped into the jungle and settled on the floor. Indiko lay siluntly at the bottom of the pit. He knew he would not be discoverd tonight, at least not by humans. After some time, Indiko became aware of a deadly silence. looking up, he seen only blackness. The blackness, houever, had a heavy breath and

A Story Within a Story (cont.)

To edit this chapter or a complete story, your checklist should include all of the elements of a story. Do the characters speak? Is the story complete? Do paragraph breaks make sense? Is the grammar correct?

the scent of the wild. The hair bristled on Indikos neck as his eyes settled on the blackest shadow in his view.   "ayaahhhh!" screemed Indiko, springing up to his one good leg and leaping upward toward the shadow. The panther growled angrily and flinched away for a moment. With new courage, it leaned back over the pit. This time, Indiko was redy. A clump of packed soil stung the panther on the nose. It bolted away again, deciding the prey in the pit was not so easy to catch. a few long, low growls echoed in the jungle, followd by the silence and then the comforting chirp of the insects.

1. Create your own checklist for a story. Use it to edit the chapter.

Checklist		
☐ _____	☐ _____	☐ _____
☐ _____	☐ _____	☐ _____
	☐ _____	☐ _____

2. Chapters often solve one conflict but leave the character with another. What conflict does this chapter resolve?
    a. Indiko falls into a trap.
    b. The panther leaves Indiko alone.
    c. The jungle tribes help Indiko.
    d. Indiko escapes from the animal pit.

3. What is Indiko's problem or conflict at the end of the chapter?
    a. The panther is trying to attack Indiko.
    b. The jungle tribes want to capture Indiko.
    c. The panther comes back to attack Indiko.
    d. Indiko is still injured and in the animal pit.

Name _____ Date _____

Vacations

Revising is not the same as editing. When you edit, you find and fix mistakes in the writing. When you **revise**, you rewrite to make the writing better. A few ways to revise are to **choose better words**, **add details**, and **combine sentences**.

Revising begins with each sentence. Here are ways to make your sentences better:

Use **vivid verbs** and use words that are more **specific**.

example: She went on vacation.

Katrina sailed on a clipper ship for three weeks through the Caribbean islands.

Combine sentences and add more details.

example: We slept in the tent. It rained all night.

The night we slept in the tent on the shores of Mirror Lake, the wind and the rain attacked our tent and kept us awake all night.

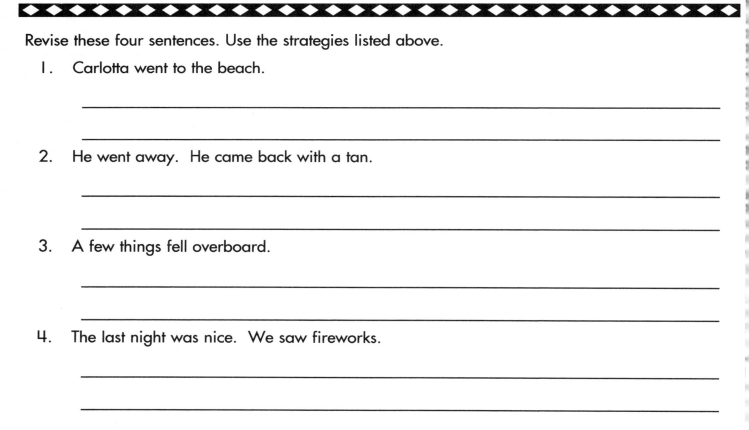

Revise these four sentences. Use the strategies listed above.

1. Carlotta went to the beach.

    _____

    _____

2. He went away. He came back with a tan.

    _____

    _____

3. A few things fell overboard.

    _____

    _____

4. The last night was nice. We saw fireworks.

    _____

    _____

Name _____ Date _____

The Main Idea

All paragraphs can be made better. To revise a paragraph, make sure that all the thoughts are about the same main idea. Vary the sentences in type and length. Revise words that repeat by finding synonyms for them. Shorten ideas that are too long or complicated. Take out sentences that don't support the main idea.

Read these paragraphs. Then revise them to make them better.

1.   Did you know there are trees under the sea? Did you know that a plant called brown algae, or kelp, is the giant of the sea? Did you know that, although the giant kelp may not look like a tree, the giant kelp has a structure like a stem with leaves that grow from the kelp's main trunk? Did you know that the giant kelp has roots that hold the kelp plant firmly to the ocean floor? The giant kelp is truly the tree of the deep.

_____

_____

_____

_____

_____

2.   Boris tucked his skis together, flew over the edge of the cliff, and landed smoothly on the slope below. Boris swished down the hill, zigzagging between trees and rocks. Boris skied well. Boris's sister, Yevni, skied even better. Boris loved to ski. Boris learned to do tricks and jumps. Boris skied in Colorado and Utah. Boris loved the soft, powdery snow. In the summer, Boris liked to hike in the mountains.

_____

_____

_____

_____

_____

113   0-7424-2755-2 *Proofreading & Editing*

Name _____ Date _____

It's Hard to Say

When revising a letter, think about the reader and focus on what the author is trying to say.

Kaitlyn is having trouble telling Ms. Fenster exactly what she means. Sometimes she repeats herself. At other times, she is simply unclear.

August 6, 2004

Dear Ms. Fenster,

　　This is a very difficult letter for me to write, especially to someone so important to me. It is hard to write to say that I will not be part of your dance class this coming year. I suppose I should tell you why I have made such a difficult choice. However, this letter is just too hard for me to write and I have to tell you that I won't be dancing with you this year. I have been invited to join a traveling dance troupe for the upcoming season. It is hard for me to write to tell you that I won't be with you this year, but I won't be able to dance in your class. I hope you know how hard this letter is to write. I won't be part of your dance class this coming year and it makes me sad.

Your student,
Kaitlyn

To revise this letter, underline the important information. Then, rewrite Kaitlyn's letter to make it better. Rewrite only the body of the letter between the greeting and closing. When you are finished, make a checklist and edit for errors in your letter.

_____

_____

_____

_____

_____

_____

_____

_____

_____

_____

_____

_____

Name _____   Date _____

Otters and Bears

Revising a newspaper article is actually quite easy. The important information is **who**, did **what**, **where**, **when**, **why**, and **how**.

Read this article. Cross out any information that does not support the title.

Otters Out-Hit Bears

In Monday's baseball game, the Ottawa Otters met the Brunswick Bears for the first time ever. The Otters scored three runs in the bottom of the eighth inning. The Bears pitcher, Chen Mun Shiew, can throw over one hundred mile per hour. The eighth-inning runs gave the Otters a two-run lead over the Bears.

In the first and third innings, Brunswick scored two runs. The Brunswick mascot, a fuzzy yellow bear, was hit with a baseball and fell to the ground. With the game all tied up, Brunswick scored again in the seventh inning. This run gave them the lead.

Wayne Albright pitched a perfect ninth inning and held the Bears scoreless. The final score was Otters—7, Bears—5. Otto, the Ottawa mascot, ran and tackled the Brunswick bear after the game was over. "It was fun to play this team," said one Ottawa player. A Brunswick player said he was delighted to play the Otters.

The team managers have agreed to play again next year in Brunswick.

Revise this article on the lines below. Include only the important information about the game. Use the facts, but make the writing interesting to the reader.

_____
_____
_____
_____
_____
_____
_____
_____
_____
_____

Name _____   Date _____

Mountain of Trash?

When you revise a report, make sure the facts are clear. Use your sentence revision skills to make the writing better. Be sure to remove any facts that are not needed for the report.

Read the first section of the report. Then follow the numbered instructions.

Mount Everest rules the earth. Mount Everest stands 29,028 feet tall. Mount Everest has been referred to as "the world's highest junkyard." Pollution is a common problem in many parts of the world. Mount Everest attracts more and more climbers who come to test their skills, but they leave behind more and more trash.

1.   One sentence does not support the main idea of this paragraph. Cross it out.

2.   Many of these sentences begin the same. Revise the paragraph to keep the reader's interest.

_____

_____

_____

_____

_____

_____

_____

_____

_____

_____

Read the next section of the report. Then follow the instructions.

Fifty tons of trash clutter the area around and on the mountain. Mount Everest is on the border between Tibet and Nepal. The people in Nepal refer to the mountain as *Sagarmatha*. That means "forehead in the sky." At the upper camps, empty oxygen bottles litter the ground. The Tibetans call the mountain "Goddess Mother of the World." Their name for the mountain is *Chomolungma*. Plastic, glass, and metal containers are strewn over the land. Over 4,000 people have tried to climb the mountain. Less than 800 have reached the peak, and more than 150 have lost their lives. Climbers often throw garbage into the huge ice crevasses. There the trash is crushed by the movement of the glacier. Years later, bits of plastic and metal come out at the bottom of the glacier.

Name _____ Date _____

Mountain of Trash? (cont.)

This paragraph gives the reader many facts about Mount Everest. Not all of these facts support the main idea of the report.

3. Circle the facts that you think best support the title "Mountain of Trash."

4. Revise the paragraph and use the facts you circled to show the reader that there is too much trash on Mount Everest.

_____

_____

_____

_____

_____

_____

_____

Read the next section of the report. Then follow the instructions.

In 1976, Nepal grew tired of people trashing the mountain. They said to the world, "Hey, cut it out!" They formed the Sagarmatha Park. The park enforces rules that will decrease the amount of garbage. Since more climbers come every year, Nepal is learning to protect its mountain.

5. The first two sentences of this paragraph use terms and language that is not right for a report. Rewrite these sentences to fit the style of the report.

_____

_____

_____

Name _____   Date _____

The "Bear" Necessities

When revising a story, make sure the writing keeps the reader's interest. Vary the types of sentences used in the story. Also, change the length of the sentences so they are not all the same.

Read the first section of the story. Then follow the instructions.

Wilt, Jolly, and Sam pulled their canoe to shore. They unloaded their gear, set up their tent, and unpacked their food. They decided to go for a hike before cooking their supper. So they left their camp and explored the rugged forests and hills. They explored for several hours before they headed back to camp.

1. This paragraph does not keep the reader's interest. One problem is that the writer only refers to Wilt, Jolly, and Sam by using the word "they." An easy way to improve writing is by finding many ways to refer to the same item, place, or people. Write at least six other ways the writer could refer to Wilt, Jolly, and Sam.

_____

_____

_____

_____

_____

_____

_____

Read the next section of the story. Then follow the instructions.

When they returned from their hike, Wilt, Jolly, and Sam were surprised because when they got back from their hike they saw three bears had moved into their camp, one of the bears was big, but two were just cubs. The mama bear was rooting through their food and one cub was chewing on Jolly's pillow and the last cub was climbing in the canoe. When Wilt, Jolly, and Sam returned to camp, they did not like what they saw, so they decided they had better sleep elsewhere and they headed for a cave they had found during their hike.

2. On a seperate piece of paper, revise this paragraph to be clear and short. Make sure the sentences are in the right order. Also, take out sentences that repeat the same idea. Remember, action is important!

     0-7424-2755-2 *Proofreading & Editing*

Name _____ Date _____

The "Bear" Necessities (cont.)

Read the next section of the story. Then follow the instructions.

The night wind rushed past the cave entrance. A thunderstorm rolled in, beating its awesome drum. A rushing wind howled across the cave opening. The wind gave a hollow, empty scream as it poured across the entrance of the cave. Rain, thunder, and lightning broke from the dark skies. Wilt, Jolly, and Sam huddled together on the hard floor. To keep warm, Wilt, Jolly, and Sam lay very close together and tried to spread Sam's jacket over all three of them. The night storm made the cave very cold.

3. This paragraph repeats ideas many times. Take out any extra information. Revise the paragraph to make it clear and short. Keep the writing interesting.

_____

_____

_____

_____

_____

_____

_____

Read the next section of the story. Then follow the instructions.

In the morning, Wilt, Jolly, and Sam went back to their camp. They didn't see any sign of the bears, so they packed everything in their canoe and went home.

4. This paragraph should be the climax of the story, but it is boring. It tells what happens, but it does not use words or actions that keep the reader interested. There is no suspense. Revise this paragraph to be more interesting. Vary the type and length of the sentences.

_____

_____

_____

_____

_____

Answer Key

Mark It, Change It
- Pages 4–5

1. When I was six, my family drove to San Francisco.
2. This time, I want to go across the Golden Gate Bridge.
3. After we see San Francisco, we are going to Los Angeles.
4. Mom says that travel helps people learn.
5. Los Angeles is huge, bright, and busy.
6. Paragraph starts with: This summer, my family and I are driving to San Francisco!
7. Aunt Maria will cook seafood for us.
8. I want to buy my mom a map of California so we can plan our trip.

Endings in Space
- Page 6

1. Kathy and Leopold entered the capsule.
2. What is their mission?
3. Look out! It's an asteroid!
4. Kathy calls back to the ship.
5. They are on their way into deep space.
6. Leopold knew that the first stay in the capsule was hard on new people. He double-checked the life-support system, placed the glass-domed helmet on his head, and locked it into place. As he nodded and moved through the airlock, Kathy closed the inner door behind him. "I guess there's no going back now, right?" she asked. Leopold just shrugged.

Mission Punctuation
- Page 7

1. Kathy ducked to enter the capsule, and Leopold followed her.
2. After a few minutes, Leopold entered the control room.
3. Kathy made sure the door was shut, locked, and secure.
4. Leopold opened a metal box, took out a connector, and plugged it in.
5. "I feel as though I'm going into a giant tin can," complained Kathy.
6. "You'll get used to it," said Leopold, "after you've been on a few trips."

The Explorers
- Page 8

1. Missing punctuation in the story includes Lewis's quotations when he talks out loud and a series in the last line of the first paragraph. Other errors include missing end marks, which are all periods.
2. Answers will vary.

The Iroquois
- Page 9

1. c
2. b
3. c
4. The Iroquois, the Mahicans, and the Wampanoag all lived in eastern America.
5. All the chiefs of the Iroquois people were at the meeting.
6. Native Americans hunted and harvested food in the fall each year.
7. We will be having a test on Friday, February 13.

8. Mr. Lehman told us about the longhouses of the Iroquois.
9. In Lancaster, Pennsylvania, the tribes met in June of 1744.
10. Benjamin Franklin read the Iroquois treaty.

Capping It Off
- Page 10

1. b
2. c
3. a
4. b
5. c
6. b
7. Our book reports are due tomorrow. I read *The Boggart* by Susan Cooper. Janna read *The Indian in the Cupboard*. Kristin liked *The Princess Bride*. There are so many great books to read! I have trouble picking just one.

The Students Vote
- Page 11

1. Capitalization errors include common nouns that are capitalized, such as music and cafeteria; days of the week and names that are not capitalized; the title "principal" capitalized when it does not appear in front of a name; and errors in capitalization in the beginning of sentences.
2. c
3. c
4. b
5. a

Spelling Counts
- Page 12

1. c
2. d
3. c
4. d
5. a
6. c
7. d
8. environment
9. community
10. history

Invisible Ink
- Page 13

1. The explanation includes a number of homophone errors, particularly to, too, and two; the word "message" is spelled correctly except in the last instance; there are other spelling mistakes throughout.
2. squeeze
3. message
4. through
5. they
6. letter
7. actual

Changing Words
- Page 14

1. a
2. c
3. c
4. a
5. b
6.–8. Answers will vary. Examples: friendly, respect, homework

Being Possessive
- Page 15

1. b
2. a
3. c
4. b
5. c
6. Did you want to go to Marisa's house?
7. How was your family's picnic?
8. I didn't know that she was Mr. Richardson's daughter!

Answer Key

John Muir, American Hero

• Page 16

1. b 3. d
2. c 4. b
5. John visited dozens of countries.
6. He began writing about nature.
7. John's writings inspired President Roosevelt to set up many national forests and parks.
8. Today, millions of people visit and enjoy wilderness areas thanks to John Muir.

The Manta Ray

• Page 17

1. Sailors saw a sea creature over twenty feet wide with horns near its head. (Answers may vary)
2. This "monster" is now known as the gentle and graceful manta ray.
3. The manta ray is one member of a large family of fish.
4. The horn shapes near the head of the manta ray guide food into its mouth.
5. The manta ray is a giant. It eats only *plankton*, tiny sea plants and animals.
6. Some people call the manta ray "the sea bat." Others call it the "devil ray."
7. The manta ray has long fins that look like wings.
8. Its tail moves like a rudder to steer the huge fish through the water.
9. Long ago, sailors thought that the manta ray was a sea monster.
10. They spotted the manta ray as it looked for food.
11. As the ray swam through shallow water, the sailors could see it.
12. I would like to see a manta ray.

The Revolution Is Now!

• Pages 18–19

1. is
2. march
3. warns
4. is
5. is
6. is
7. is
8. My brother joins (or joined) the fighting at Concord.
9. We worry about him as he fights for freedom.
10. Colonists help each other with food and information.
11. b
12. b
13. a
14. John Paul Jones was a great commander.
15. General Nathanael Green led the army in the South.
16. Lafayette helped the troops after he arrived from France.
17. Yorktown was the last major battle of the war.
18. Cornwallis surrendered on October 19, 1782.
19. The Treaty of Paris was signed in 1783.
20. The brave colonists were now Americans.
21. Answers will vary.

Arachne

• Pages 20–21

1. Long ago in a distant country lived a young woman named Arachne.
2. Arachne wove the most beautiful cloth anyone had ever seen.
3. Everyone in Arachne's village talked about her wonderful cloth, and soon she became famous.
4. But as her fame grew, so did her pride.
5. "I am the best weaver in the world," Arachne boasted.
6. She said, "Not even the goddess Minerva could make anything so fine."
7. Minerva wove cloth for all the gods.
8. She was proud of her weaving and thought that no human could ever match her skills.
9. Soon Arachne's words reached Minerva's ears and the goddess became angry.
10. Minerva called to Arachne and challenged her to a contest.
11. a
12. b
13. a
14. The paragraphs have errors with possessives, verb tenses, missing words, word order, and subject-verb agreement.

The Pilgrims

• Page 22

1. The Pilgrims sailed from Plymouth, England, on the *Mayflower* on September 6, 1620.
2. There were 102 passengers on board.
3. The beginning of the voyage was pleasant.
4. But then the ship ran into storms and high winds.
5. Beams on deck cracked and let water leak into the ship.
6. Two adults died on the voyage, and one baby was born. He was named "Oceanus."
7. On November 9, 1620, the *Mayflower* neared land.
8. It was where Cape Cod is now.
9. Two days later, after 66 days at sea, the ship dropped its anchor.
10. Some of the Pilgrims went ashore.
11. Now we remember their first harvest celebration on Thanksgiving Day.

Buster

• Page 23

1. Mistakes in the letter include misspellings, capitalization errors, one missing end mark, errors in the heading, opening, and closing.
2. Answers will vary.

Poets

• Page 24

1. S 4. F
2. S 5. S
3. F 6. F
7. His poems are silly and fun.
8. His poems are set in New England.

Answer Key

Animals in the City
Page 25
1. Everyone knows that animals and birds live in the forest. They also live in cities.
2. Squirrels live in trees on city streets. Rabbits and opossums make their homes in the wide-open spaces of city parks.
3. Everyone has seen pigeons in the city. They love to flock near fountains and food stands.
4. Mice make their nests in apartments. Rats find all sorts of hiding places for homes.
5. Raccoons search for food in garbage cans at night, and foxes come out at night, too.

Paul Revere
• **Page 26**
1. C
2. S
3. CX
4. S
5. C
6. CX
7. S
8. S
9. C
10. CX

The Fourth of July
Page 27
1. I (circled) like the Fourth of July.(underlined)
2. The red, white, and blue colors (circled) are so bright.(underlined)
3. My family and I (circled) like the parade the best.(underlined)
4. Even though we (circled) like the band music (underlined), we (circled) also like the barbecue after the parade.(underlined)
5. We (circled) always have to wait our turn when we get to the food stand. (underlined)
6. I (circled) like the hamburgers the best (underlined) even though I (circled) also like hot dogs.(underlined)
7. The first song (circled) is happy (underlined), but the second song (circled) sounds sad. (underlined)
8. It (circled) reminds Dad of his army friends (underlined), and Mom (circled) puts her arm around him.(underlined)
9. It (circled) is time for the fireworks (underlined), and I (circled) can hardly wait! (underlined)

Pictures in the Mind
• **Page 28**
Answers will vary. Examples:
1. screamed
2. paced
3. skipped
4. shone
5. sobbed
6. sunny
7. crawls
8. sultry
9. banged
10. exhausted

It's Like This
• **Page 29**
1.–15. Answers will vary.

Lady Liberty
• **Page 30**
1. b
2. b
3. Answers will vary.
4. a,d

On Topic
• **Page 31**
1. f
2. a
3. h
4. c
5. i
6. d
7. b
8. e
9. g

Deep Waters
• **Page 32**
1. a, b, d
2. a, c, e
3. a, c, d

Beautiful Buildings
• **Page 33**
1. b
2. c
3. a

A Famous Writer
Pages 34–35
1. c
2. d
3. b
4. a

Paragraph Power
• **Page 36**
1. c
2. b
3. c

A Mysterious Island
• **Page 37**
Paragraphs begin with the first sentence; with "Archaeologists now believe. . ."; and with "Today, Easter Island. . ." Sentences that don't belong: "The Dutch have always been famous for their seagoing adventures." "There were also extinct volcanoes on the island." "Cannibals also lived at that time in Indonesia." "Other countries in South America include Paraguay and Peru."

Answer Key

Fire!
• Page 38

The story should be marked with a new paragraph for each new character's line of dialogue.

The Amazing Mozart
• Page 39

Order of sentences: 3, 9, 7, 10, 1, 13, 11, 6, 2, 5, 12, 8, 4
Students should underline these as topic sentences:
(1) Wolfgang Amadeus Mozart was born in 1756 in Austria.
(5) When Mozart became an adult, he moved to Vienna and married.
(9) Toward the end of his life, Mozart began working on a piece called "Requiem."

Walking a Thin Line
• Page 40

Order of paragraphs: 3, 1, 5, 4, 2

Strong Arguments
• Page 41
1. b
2. a
3.–4. Answers will vary. Make sure that reasons support the opinion.

Tons of Trash
• Page 42

The essay contains errors in spelling, capitalization, and a few punctuation errors, including apostrophes. Paragraphs should be marked at the first sentence; at "Garbologists, garbage scientists…"; and at "Someday, we may be able…"

Talking About Topics
• Page 43
1. b
2. b
3. c
4. c
5. Answers will vary.

Titles Are Telling
• Page 44
1. b
2. c
3. b
4. c
5.–6. Answers will vary.

The Right Topics
• Page 45
1. b
2. d
3. b
4. d
5. b
6. b

A Sense of Purpose
• Page 46
1. b
2. e
3. c
4. d
5. a
6. f

Hear, Hear!
• Page 47
1. c
2. a
3. c

The Best Words
• Pages 48–49
1. b
2. b
3. c
4. b
5. a
6. b
7. c
8.–13. Answers will vary. Examples (words to be removed in parentheses):
8. (cute)   tough
9. (sour)   salty
10. (faint)   determined
11. (searched) explored
12. (papery)   athletic
13. (amusing)   algebra
14. Answers will vary.
15. Words students should delete: small, birds, fewest, hate. Examples of replacement words: intelligent, animals, greatest, want

Word Choices
• Page 50
1. a
2. b
3. b
4. a

A World of Ice
• Page 51
1. Examples of words to take out: above, popular, swimming, not, people, forgotten, silly. Words should be replaced with appropriate choices.
2. a
3. b
4. b

It Fits
• Pages 52–53
1. a
2. c
3. b
4. a
5.–10. Answers will vary.

Answer Key

Summing It Up
• Page 54
1. People have always looked to the heavens for clues to the world around them.
2. Several track runners have proven their super speed by racing 50 meters against horses.
3. d
4. c

Can You Paraphrase?
• Page 55
1. a
2. b

Go to the Source!
• Page 56
1. a
2. c
3. c
4. a
5. Answers will vary. Examples: periodicals, Internet sites, public television shows
6. Answers will vary. Examples: a book about daily life in Ecuador or an encyclopedia article about the country

Runaway Buffalo
• Page 57
Underlined phrases: Chan (should be Chen); rowed (should be canoed or paddled); north (should be south); Park rangers had no idea that the buffalo had gone to the island (should be Park rangers knew that the buffalo had gone to the island, but thought it was no longer there); swimming back to shore (should be canoed back to shore)

A Report About George
• Pages 58–59
Underlined phrases: 1733 (should be 1732); surveyor for Westmoreland County (should be Culpepper County); He survived having a horse shot out from underneath him (should be two horses); 1776 (should be 1775) Constitutional Convention in 1789 (should be 1787); Washington retired in 1799 (should be died in 1799)
1. biography of Washington or encyclopedia article
2. encyclopedia or Internet resource
3. dictionary
4. Answers will vary.

Eyewitness Reports
• Pages 60–61
1. a stage
2. white spacesuit, helmet with shiny black glass
3. no, because Erin Thompson wasn't scared
4. an actor from the play
5.–9. Rewritten sentences will vary. Students should underline: at one end of the mall (should be in the center of the mall); This started a panic as terrified shoppers fled the mall (this was not verified by all reports); after the alien grabbed her (Justina never said that); "The situation is now back to normal." (should be the situation is now under control); "Blasting Off" (should be "Blast Off!")

Life in Australia
• Pages 62–63
1. b or c
2. b
3. a
4. b
5. b

The Right Tool
Pages 64–65
1. all
2. b, d
3. a
4. a, b, d, e
5. a, b, d
6. Students should find errors in spelling, capitalization, and punctuation.
7. a, c, d
8. d
9. Students should find two paragraph breaks, three errors in capitalization, an error with a comma and with a quotation mark.

I'm Sorry
Page 66
1. Editing focus is on punctuation, spelling, and indenting. Students should notice errors in the heading and closing (opening is correct).
2. a, b, d

Letter to the Editor
Page 67
1. Editing focus is on punctuation, spelling, and indenting. Students should notice errors in the heading, opening, and closing.
2. c

A Business Deal
Pages 68–69
1. c
2. No. Explanations will vary, but should include the fact that until Laur had sold the quilts, she would not be able to calculate the profits.
3. d
4. Editing focus is on spelling, punctuation, and capitalization.
5. c
6. because there are no quotes in this report

A Journey in History
Pages 70–71
1. a fictional story set in a real time and place in history
2. *Number the Stars* by Lois Lowry
3. She wanted to save her Jewish friend from the Nazis.
4. b
5. Annemarie had a sister named Lise.
   The Jews in Poland were also tormented.
6. b
7. Editing focus is on spelling, punctuation, and indenting. Students should notice a number a capitalization errors of proper names and place names. They should correct verb tense and forms of irregular verbs.

Answer Key

Do You See the Problem?
Pages 72–73
1. 250,000 Asian children (source 1)
   no tuna (source 2)
2. a
3. The health of a child's bones is very important.
4. Editing focus is on spelling, capitalization, indenting. Students should carefully check the facts against the sources.

The End of an Empire
Pages 74–75
1. Editing focus is on spelling, capitalization, and grammar. Students should use the questions to guide them to check all of the facts against the timeline and the map.
2. d
3. b

A Heritage Report
Pages 76–77
1. b
2. Italy
3. Answers will vary.
4. There is a famous tower there that leans over.
5. Editing focuses on capitalization of proper nouns, spelling, and indenting.

On Top of Mount Rosa
Pages 78–79
1. Editing focus is on punctuation, capitalization, and spelling. If students use another type of format for science experiment reports, they could use the data from this report and rework it into their preferred format.
2. d

Nothing but Trouble
Pages 80–81
1. The townspeople were concerned that the McKenzie twins would cause some disaster.
2. They did cause a disaster, but everyone survived; when the cake crumbled, the flood waters receded.
3. Answers will vary. Students can use other transitions, alter sentences, or cut out the word *unfortunately* without replacing it.
4. Editing focus is on spelling, punctuation, capitalization (especially of proper names), and indenting. Students could transfer their rewrites from question 3 into the actual text of the story.

Operation Sleep-In
Pages 82–83
1. Editing focus is on indenting and quotation marks. There are also spelling errors and other punctuation errors in the story.
2. Answers will vary but should solve the conflict of Jessica's offense. Students might also have Miss Loudmont realize that she needs to compromise because of the actions of the girls.

The Journal of Juan Ponce de León
Pages 84–85
1. Editing focus is on spelling, grammar, and punctuation. There are subject-verb agreement errors, mistakes in series of commas, and a number of spelling errors.
2. A journal is only one person's point of view; journals are in chronological order, journals are dated
3. b
4. c
5. Answers will vary.

Live Concert!
Pages 86–87
1. Editing focus is on quotations from various characters, indenting for new paragraphs, capitalization, and spelling errors.
2. a, d
3. Trevor, Veronica, and the speaker were attending a live concert for Oxygen for All and wanted to go backstage to meet the band.
4. b, c, e, f

Achoo!
Page 88
1. A
2. Editing should focus on the items listed in checklist A.

The Wheelchair
Page 89
Editing focus is on spelling, punctuation, capitalization, and grammar, including a double negative and subject-verb agreement errors.

Time Machines in the Attic
Pages 90–91
1. Editing focus is on spelling, capitalization, and punctuation. There are some challenging words in this poem; encourage students to check them in a dictionary.
2. c
3. d
4. a
5. c
6. b
7. d

Answer Key

Back to Basics
Pages 92–93
1. Although
2. their
3. great, piece
4. again
5. c
6. On July 20, 1969, an American was the first person to step on the moon.
7. We used to live in Dallas, Texas, at 772 Congress Drive.
8. "There is no heat," Rico noted at midday. "It is still 15 degrees below zero."
9. d
10. a
11. d
12. After hearing the instructions, we still didn't know how to drive to Dr. Kirk's house.
13. Mr. Ingham studied at Hiram Law School in Standsbury, Connecticut.
14. all
15. b
16. c

Yours, Mine, Theirs, or Ours?
Page 94
2. Becky's house
3. the cold war's place in history
4. the players' score
5. the baby's shoes
6. the children's game
7. Alea's cat
8. Mrs. Marx's car
9. the city's bus
10. students'
11. Shireen's
12. cats'

Remember the Alamo!
Page 95
1. c
2. a
3. b
4. c
5. entered
6. demanded
7. see, gave
8. came
9. Wouldn't it be wonderful if the walls of the Alamo could tell their secrets?
10. Dad asked me if I thought that I would have been brave enough to fight.
11. I'm not sure, but I imagine I would be as courageous as the heroes of the Alamo.
12. I will always remember our incredible trip!

A High-Tech Gift of Memories
Page 96
1. a
2. c
3. fragment; students must edit to make it a complete sentence
4. The next step is to put the pictures in the order they choose.
5. The technology makes this step very easy.
6. Once the images are in order, transitions are added.
7. The transitions move from one picture to another in a pleasing way.
8. Sound creation is next. They record music that they play.
9. Once the recording is finished, they link the sound with the pictures.
10. Movie technology helped Matti and Kim create a very special gift for their parents.
    or, With movie technology, Matti and Kim created a very special gift for their parents.

A Trip to Diver's Cove
Page 97
1. complex, Putting on her snorkel and mask, Jennifer explored the cove.
2. fragment, Answers will vary.
3. run-on, her. They, or her, and they
4. simple, Suddenly, Jennifer saw something moving.
5. complex, Motioning to her brother, Jennifer looked more closely.
6. compound, One tentacle rose, and another appeared.
7. simple, A miniature octopus peeked at the children.
8. complex, Just as suddenly as it appeared, it disappeared!
9. fragment, Answers will vary.
10. d

The Spice of Life!
Page 98
1.–3. Answers will vary.
4. As it broke into the earth's atmosphere, the meteor split the darkness of night.

One Idea at a Time
Page 99
1. a
2. a
3. c

What's the Point?
Page 100
1. c
2. b
3. c
4. a
5. b
6.–7. Answers will vary.

Tell Me Why
Page 101
1. b
2. c
3. a
4. Answers will vary.
5. Answers will vary.

Answer Key

Splasher
Page 102
Checklist should include: commas after greeting and closing, comma between date and year, spelling, punctuation, capitalization, indenting, and grammar. Editing focus is on spelling and punctuation, with mistakes in capitalization of proper names.

A Letter Home
Page 103
Checklist should include: commas after greeting and closing, comma between date and year, spelling, punctuation, capitalization, indenting, and grammar. Editing focus is on indenting, capitalization, and punctuation. Students should notice capitalization errors with proper names and a homophone error in the last line of the letter. There are mistakes in the heading and closing, but not in the opening.

The Road to Wonderland
Pages 104–105
1. Checklist should include: facts match the source material, topic sentences and details, spelling, punctuation, capitalization, indenting, and grammar. Editing focus is on spelling, punctuation, and capitalization. Students should notice that <u>Alice's Adventure in Wonderland</u>, because it is a book title, should be underlined rather than appear in quotation marks.
2. c
3. b
4. c

One Problem or Another
Pages 106–107
1. a
2. Answers will vary. Bill, not Marquita, said that it would be worse (not better) if someone had to go hungry. Delete the second-to-last sentence.
3. Last sentence could tie in more strongly with the opening thoughts and talk about a change that helps address the problem specifically.
4. Checklist should include: facts match the source material, topic sentences and details, spelling, punctuation, capitalization, indenting, and grammar. Editing focus is on spelling, punctuation, and capitalization.

Peace, At All Costs
Pages 108–109
1. on a battlefield long ago
2. Reginald's and Arnold's armies plan to fight, but Reginald wants peace.
3. b
4. Arnold agrees to peace with the concessions Reginald makes.
5. c
6. Checklist should include: spelling, grammar, capitalization, punctuation, story elements, quotation marks, indenting. Editing focus is on paragraph breaks and quotation marks.

A Story Within a Story
Pages 110–111
1. Checklist should include: spelling, grammar, capitalization, punctuation, story elements, quotations, indenting. Editing focus is on paragraph breaks; students cannot rely on speeches by characters to indicate breaks because there is only one line of dialogue. Students will find some spelling, capitalization, and punctuation errors.
2. b
3. d

Vacations
Page 112
1.–4. Answers will vary. All answers should employ one or more of the techniques discussed: vivid verbs, specific details, combining sentences, and adding more detail.

The Main Idea
Page 113
1.– 2. Answers will vary, but sentences should be much shorter so that students can combine them and vary the sentence structure.

It's Hard to Say
Page 114
Delete repetition. Final version should be clear and concise.

Otters and Bears
Page 115
Answers will vary. All facts should be about the baseball game, so article will be much shorter. Students should eliminate extraneous information, such as the information about the mascots.

Mountain of Trash
Pages 116–117
1. crossed-out sentence: Pollution is a common problem in many parts of the world.
2. Students should vary the sentence structure in their revision.
3. Circled facts should include the amount of trash and types of trash found on the mountain. Students may choose to keep the total number of hikers, but the number of hikers who have reached the peak or died is irrelevant to the topic.
4. Revision should be based on facts that students have circled.
5. Students should use appropriate language to convey the idea of Nepal's government forming a park to enforce rules to eliminate littering.

The "Bear" Necessities
Pages 118–119
1. Answers will vary. Examples: the boys, the campers, the three friends, the young men, etc.
2.–4. Answers will vary. Be sure that students follow the specific instructions of each section in their revisions.

Proofreading Marks

Capitalize a letter: w.

bilbo baggins

Lowercase a letter: D̸.

H̸ouse

Delete a letter or a word: ℒ.

the ~~the~~ big ogre.

Change the order of letters or words: ∩ .

recieve

Add a word, a period, a comma or other punctuation: ⌄ ⌄ ⌄.

of
The Lord ⌃ the Rings

Show start of a new paragraph: ¶ .

That's why I really like astronomy. ¶Another favorite pasttime I have is studying dinosaurs. My collection of dinosaur resources includes several books, models, and a real fossil I found while visiting Arizona.